Exploring Alternate Realities Through Parallel Worlds

Exploring Alternate Realities Through Parallel Worlds

Mack Rafeal

UNIEK ENTERPRISES

CONTENTS

INDEX

Chapter 1

Introduction

The idea of substitute real factors and equal universes has long caught the human creative mind. From old legends to current sci-fi, the possibility that there might be different aspects or domains that exist close by our own has been a wellspring of interest and hypothesis. This interest has prompted a rich embroidery of stories, hypotheses, and methods of reasoning, all revolved around equal universes and substitute real factors. In this investigation, we leave on an excursion to comprehend the different features of this captivating idea and the manners by which it has penetrated our social and logical stories.

At the core of equal universes lies the thought that there are different, unmistakable real factors that exist in lined up with our own, each with its own one of a kind qualities, occasions, and conceivable outcomes. These universes can go from being unobtrusively unique in relation to our own to completely different concerning actual regulations, authentic occasions, and, surprisingly, the idea of reality itself. The thought that there could be elective adaptations of our reality, where various decisions were made, and various results came about, brings up significant issues about the idea of the real world and the conceivable outcomes that lie past our ongoing getting it.

Equal universes isn't bound to a solitary social or scholarly custom. It very well may be tracked down in different structures across various human advancements and verifiable periods. In antiquated folklore, there are various stories of extraordinary domains, for example, the Greek idea of Gehenna or the Norse confidence in domains like Asgard and Midgard. These domains frequently filled in as clarifications for the secrets of life, passing, and the great beyond, and they were accepted to exist close by the human world.

In later history, the idea of equal universes has been investigated in writing and craftsmanship. Crafted by creators like Lewis Carroll, with his "Alice's Experiences in Wonderland," and L. Straightforward Baum, with his "The Wizard of Oz" series, acquainted perusers with fantastical universes that existed lined up with our own. These accounts tested the limits of the real world and the impediments of human discernment, welcoming perusers to examine the chance of different domains past their ordinary encounters.

Equal universes have likewise assumed a huge part in philosophical idea. The rationalist Friedrich Nietzsche, for example, presented the possibility of the "everlasting repeat," recommending that each occasion in the universe repeats a boundless number of times in an endless number of equal universes. This idea brings up issues about the idea of presence, through and through freedom, and the certainty of our activities.

As we dive further into the investigation of equal universes, we experience the idea's significant effect on contemporary sci-fi. The class has been a prolific ground for the assessment of substitute real factors and equal universes, frequently filling in as a stage for resolving complex philosophical and moral inquiries. Journalists like Philip K. Dick, in his book "The Man in the High Palace," and Michael Moorcock, in his "Everlasting Hero" series, have woven mind boggling accounts that investigate the results of various authentic results and the presence of different real factors.

Also, the appearance of present day physical science has brought equal universes into the domain of logical request. Quantum mechanics, a basic hypothesis in physical science, recommends that particles can exist in numerous states all the while until they are noticed, leading to the idea of the multiverse. As per this hypothesis, there might be incalculable equal universes, each with its own arrangement of actual regulations and constants. These universes might actually go from those almost indistinguishable from our own to tremendously various ones where the laws of physical science as we comprehend them don't make a difference.

The idea of the multiverse opens up a huge range of potential outcomes and difficulties our crucial comprehension of the universe and our place inside it. It brings up issues about the idea of the real world, the presence of other smart life, and the potential for movement between these equal universes.

One of the most fascinating parts of equal universes is the possibility that they could offer a departure from the impediments and imperatives of our own existence. In writing and film, the idea of equal universes has frequently been utilized for of wish-satisfaction or as a method for investigating the outcomes of various decisions. The possibility that there may be a variant of reality where our fantasies have materialized or where we settled on various life changing choices is both charming and interesting.

However, the charm of equal universes goes past simple idealism. It takes advantage of our firmly established interest in the obscure and the neglected. It mixes our longing to wander past the limits of our ongoing information and to look for replies to the most significant inquiries concerning presence. Equal universes offer a tempting look into the endless conceivable outcomes that might exist past our ongoing comprehension of the real world.

Equal universes likewise give an interesting focal point through which to look at the idea of human life and our decisions. The possibility that our activities in a single world could have expansive results in one more moves us to think about the moral and moral elements of our choices. It prompts us to ponder the interconnectedness of all life and the expected effect of our decisions on the texture of the multiverse.

Besides, equal universes offer a fruitful ground for investigating the idea of character. On the off chance that there are endless variants of ourselves in equal universes, each with various encounters and results, what's the significance here to be "us"? Might it be said that we are characterized by our decisions, our conditions, or our inborn characteristics? These inquiries challenge how we might interpret self as well as welcome us to consider the idea of choice and determinism.

In the domain of sci-fi, the idea of equal universes has been bridled to investigate the moral ramifications of cutting edge innovation, for example, equal universe travel or the making of counterfeit real factors. These accounts frequently act as wake up calls, advance notice us about the possible results of altering the limits of the real world. They help us to remember the requirement for mindful and moral utilization of innovation, particularly with regards to how we might interpret equal universes.

Equal universes are not restricted to the domain of sci-fi or reasoning; they have additionally tracked down their direction into different otherworldly and mysterious practices. The confidence in supernatural domains or planes of presence is a typical subject in numerous religions and conviction frameworks. These domains are frequently viewed as where the spirit might pursue passing or where profound creatures live. At times, people might try to associate with these equal universes through contemplation, custom, or other profound practices.

Equal universes has likewise gotten forward momentum with regards to quantum cognizance and the investigation of adjusted conditions of mindfulness. A few specialists and logicians recommend that our view of the truth isn't restricted to a solitary, fixed aspect however can be changed and extended to incorporate different domains of cognizance. This point of view brings up issues about the idea of human insight and the limits of how we might interpret reality.

As of late, the idea of equal universes has even advanced into mainstream society and amusement in different structures, including TV series, computer games, and augmented reality encounters. These mediums permit crowds to drench themselves in equal universes and investigate the boundless potential outcomes they offer. As innovation keeps on propelling, the limit between the virtual and the genuine foggy spots, and the investigation of substitute real factors turns out to be more open and enrapturing.

While the idea of equal universes is without a doubt enrapturing, it likewise raises various difficulties and Catch 22s. One of the most notable is the purported "butterfly impact," a term begat in disorder hypothesis, which proposes that little changes in a single world could have broad and flighty outcomes in another. This thought highlights the complicated interchange among circumstances and logical results and the inborn unconventionality of the multiverse.

The idea of equal universes additionally brings up issues about the idea of perception and estimation. In quantum mechanics, the demonstration of perception is fundamental to the hypothesis, yet it stays hazy how perception could function with regards to resemble universes. On the off chance that each conceivable result of an occasion happens in various equal universes, how does perception influence the truth we experience, and what's the significance here to "notice" in a multiverse?

Additionally, the actual presence of equal universes challenges the idea of uniqueness and peculiarity. Assuming there are boundless equal universes, each with its own arrangement of occasions and results, does the idea of uniqueness lose its importance? How might we grasp the boundlessness and variety of the multiverse without reducing the meaning of our own world?

The investigation of equal universes likewise presents a test with regards to experimental proof. While equal universes is a dazzling idea in principle, giving exact proof or exploratory verification has been testing. A significant number of the cases about equal universes are established in hypothetical physical science and math, making it challenging to test their legitimacy in a conventional logical sense.

In any case, the shortfall of observational proof doesn't reduce the scholarly and philosophical worth of the idea of equal universes. It keeps on filling in as a strong structure for investigating the constraints of human figuring out, the idea of the real world, and the significant inquiries regarding presence. The shortfall of authoritative evidence just adds to the persona and charm of the idea, leaving space for proceeded exploration.

1.1 Introduction to the concept of parallel worlds

Equal universes, substitute real factors, or different aspects has long captivated mankind. An idea has pervaded folklores, writing, reasoning, and, surprisingly, the domain of current science. These equal universes are imagined as isolated, coinciding real factors that might fluctuate from somewhat various variants of our own reality to fundamentally unmistakable domains represented by substitute laws of material science and history. The appeal of equal universes lies in their capability to open new points of view on the real world, offering the enticing possibility of investigating the immense obscure that exists past the limits of our ongoing comprehension.

Equal universes, frequently alluded to as resemble universes or substitute real factors, have tracked down their place in different social and scholarly customs. They aren't restricted to a particular period or locale however are a repetitive subject in human idea. In antiquated folklores, we track down accounts of powerful domains, like the Greek hidden world of Abbadon or the Norse domains of Asgard and Midgard. These domains filled in as clarifications for the secrets of life, demise, and eternity, offering bits of knowledge into the human condition and the idea of presence itself.

Equal universes additionally show up noticeably in the domain of writing and craftsmanship. Famous creators like Lewis Carroll, in "Alice's Experiences in Wonderland," and L. Straightforward Baum, in his "The Wizard of Oz" series, shipped perusers to fantastical universes that coincided with our own. These stories tested the actual idea of the real world, welcoming perusers to investigate the limits of human discernment and think about the presence of different aspects past our ordinary encounters.

Additionally, the idea of equal universes has transformed the domain of reasoning. The savant Friedrich Nietzsche presented the idea of the "timeless repeat," recommending that each occasion in the universe repeats limitlessly in endless equal universes. This idea brings up significant issues about the idea of presence, through and through freedom, and the certainty of human activities. It prompts us to mull over the interconnectedness of all life and the effect of our decisions on the amazing embroidery of presence.

Equal universes have fundamentally impacted contemporary sci-fi, giving a rich source to investigating complex philosophical and moral inquiries. Creators like Philip K. Dick, in his book "The Man in the High Palace," and Michael Moorcock, with his "Everlasting Hero" series, have woven complicated accounts that analyze the repercussions of various verifiable results and the presence of numerous real factors. These works challenge perusers to consider the results of disparate ways and the complexities of reality itself.

Besides, the appearance of present day physical science has brought the idea of equal universes into the domain of logical request. Quantum mechanics, a primary hypothesis in physical science, suggests that particles can exist in various states all the while until noticed, consequently leading to the idea of the multiverse. As per this hypothesis, there might exist innumerable equal universes, each administered by its own arrangement of actual regulations and constants. These universes can go from intently looking like our own to profoundly various ones where the laws of material science, as we comprehend them, never again apply.

The possibility of the multiverse broadens the extent of conceivable outcomes and difficulties our key cognizance of the universe and our place inside it. It brings up significant issues about the idea of the real world, the presence of other keen life, and the potential for crossing between these equal universes.

One of the most fascinating parts of equal universes is the idea that they could offer a departure from the restrictions and imperatives of our own existence. In writing and film, equal universes have frequently filled in for the purpose of wish-satisfaction or as a stage for investigating the outcomes of various decisions. The chance of different real factors where our fantasies are understood or where we pursued unmistakable life changing choices is both tempting and provocative.

However, the appeal of equal universes rises above simple idealism. It takes advantage of mankind's firmly established interest in the obscure and the unfamiliar. It lights our craving to wander past the limits of our ongoing information and to look for replies to the most significant inquiries concerning presence. Equal universes offer a tempting look into the limitless conceivable outcomes that might exist past our ongoing comprehension of the real world.

Besides, equal universes give a remarkable focal point through which we can inspect the idea of human life and our decisions. The possibility that our activities in a single world might have expansive results in one more prompts us to mull over the moral and moral elements of our choices. It urges us to ponder the interconnectedness of all life and the likely effect of our decisions on the texture of the multiverse.

Equal universes likewise offer a ripe ground for investigating the idea of character. Assuming there are endless renditions of ourselves in equal universes, each with various encounters and results, what's the significance here to be "us"? Is it safe to say that we are characterized by our decisions, our conditions, or our innate characteristics? These inquiries challenge how we might interpret self as well as welcome us to contemplate the idea of freedom of thought and determinism.

In the domain of sci-fi, the idea of equal universes has been tackled to investigate the moral ramifications of trend setting innovation, for example, equal universe travel or the making of fake real factors. These accounts frequently act as wake up calls, advance notice us about the possible results of altering the limits of the real world. They help us to remember the requirement for capable and moral utilization of innovation, particularly with regards to how we might interpret equal universes.

Equal universes are not restricted to the domain of sci-fi or reasoning; they have likewise tracked down their direction into different otherworldly and magical customs. The faith in extraordinary domains or planes of presence is a typical subject in numerous religions and conviction frameworks. These domains are frequently viewed as where the spirit might pursue passing or where otherworldly creatures dwell. At times, people might look to interface with these equal universes through reflection, custom, or other profound practices.

Equal universes has likewise built up forward momentum with regards to quantum cognizance and the investigation of changed conditions of mindfulness. A few scientists and logicians recommend that our view of the truth isn't restricted to a solitary, fixed aspect however can be changed and extended to incorporate different domains of cognizance. This point of view brings up issues about the idea of human discernment and the limits of how we might interpret reality.

Lately, the idea of equal universes has even advanced into mainstream society and diversion in different structures, including TV series, computer games, and augmented reality encounters.

These mediums permit crowds to drench themselves in equal universes and investigate the boundless potential outcomes they offer. As innovation keeps on propelling, the limit between the virtual and the genuine hazy spots, and the investigation of substitute real factors turns out to be more available and spellbinding.

While the idea of equal universes is without a doubt enamoring, it likewise raises various difficulties and Catch 22s. One of the most notable is the purported "butterfly impact," a term begat in disorder hypothesis, which recommends that little changes in a single world could have broad and unusual outcomes in another. This thought highlights the complicated exchange among circumstances and logical results and the inborn flightiness of the multiverse.

The idea of equal universes likewise brings up issues about the idea of perception and estimation. In quantum mechanics, the demonstration of perception is key to the hypothesis, yet it stays muddled how perception could function with regards to resemble universes. On the off chance that each conceivable result of an occasion happens in various equal universes, how does perception influence the truth we experience, and what's the significance here to "notice" in a multiverse?

Besides, the actual presence of equal universes challenges the idea of uniqueness and peculiarity. Assuming there are boundless equal universes, each with its own arrangement of occasions and results, does the idea of uniqueness lose its significance? How might we understand the tremendousness and variety of the multiverse without decreasing the meaning of our own existence?

The investigation of equal universes likewise presents a test regarding experimental proof. While equal universes is an enthralling idea in principle, giving exact proof or trial verification has been testing. A considerable lot of the cases about equal universes are established in hypothetical physical science and math, making it hard to test their legitimacy in a conventional logical sense.

In any case, the shortfall of exact proof doesn't reduce the scholarly and philosophical worth of the idea of equal universes. It keeps on filling in as a strong structure for investigating the constraints of human figuring out, the idea of the real world, and the significant inquiries concerning presence. The shortfall of authoritative confirmation just adds to the persona and appeal of the idea, leaving space for proceeded with investigation and hypothesis.

1.2 Historical and cultural perspectives on alternate realities

The idea of substitute real factors, equal universes, or different aspects is definitely not a new innovation however has profound verifiable and social roots. All through mankind's set of experiences, various developments and conviction frameworks have wrestled with the possibility that there may be real factors past the one we see. These verifiable and social points of view on substitute real factors give significant bits of knowledge into how human social orders have considered the obscure and the baffling all through the ages.

In the old world, substitute real factors frequently tracked down articulation in fanciful and strict stories. Many societies trusted in the presence of powerful domains possessed by divine beings, spirits, or otherworldly creatures. In Greek folklore, for example, the hidden world, managed by Gehenna, was an unmistakable substitute reality that housed the spirits of the departed. These legends offered clarifications for the secrets of life, demise, and the hereafter, giving a structure to understanding the change starting with one reality then onto the next.

In Hinduism, the idea of the multiverse is profoundly imbued, with convictions in numerous domains or Lokas. These Lokas exist close by our reality, each with its own exceptional attributes and occupants. The possibility of numerous planes of presence in Hindu cosmology mirrors a rich social and otherworldly custom that recognizes the presence of substitute real factors.

Essentially, the Norse cosmology portrayed an intricate arrangement of domains, including Midgard (the human world) and Asgard (the domain of the divine beings). The faith in these equal universes was necessary to Norse folklore and affected the perspective of the Viking public.

In old Egypt, the excursion to the great beyond was a focal part of strict conviction. The Egyptians had confidence in an equal reality where the spirit would be judged and, whenever viewed as commendable, would proceed to a timeless presence within the sight of the divine beings. The possibility of an equal domain of presence past death was a principal part of Egyptian culture.

These old convictions in substitute real factors filled in as a method for figuring out the world, its secrets, and the human experience. They gave a structure to understanding the changes between various conditions, like life and demise, and offered a brief look into the significant inquiries regarding the idea of presence.

Notwithstanding folklore and religion, the idea of substitute real factors has been a repetitive subject in writing and workmanship. These inventive articulations have permitted social orders to investigate the limits of human creative mind and to contemplate the potential outcomes of equal universes. The stories of substitute real factors in writing have frequently worked as both diversion and psychological studies, testing the shows of the real world.

One of the most renowned early attempts to investigate substitute truths is Lewis Carroll's "Alice's Experiences in Wonderland." In this eccentric story, Alice coincidentally finds a fantastical world that resists the laws of physical science and rationale. The account welcomes perusers to consider the constraints of the real world and the idea that substitute aspects could exist close by our own.

Similarly, L. Honest Baum's "The Wizard of Oz" acquainted perusers with the Place where there is Oz, a spot that exists together with the commonplace world yet is loaded up with supernatural animals and captivating undertakings. Baum's innovative world enraptured the creative mind of perusers and established the groundwork for a progression of equal world stories.

Equal universes have likewise showed up with regards to philosophical idea. Friedrich Nietzsche presented the idea of the "everlasting repeat," proposing that each occasion in the universe repeats a limitless number of times. This idea brings up issues about the idea of presence, through and through freedom, and the certainty of human activities. Nietzsche's thoughts tested traditional philosophical idea and empowered consideration of the possible presence of equal real factors.

As we travel through history, the idea of substitute real factors proceeds to develop and take on new structures. The nineteenth and twentieth hundreds of years saw a flood in sci-fi writing and speculative fiction, which frequently investigated the topic of equal universes. Creators like H.G. Wells, with his book "The Conflict of the Universes," and Jules Verne, with "Excursion to the Focal point of the Earth," acquainted perusers with substitute aspects and universes concealed underneath the outer layer of the Earth.

Equal universes have likewise been entwined with the cutting edge interest with the extraordinary and the paranormal. Ideas like apparitions, spirits, and hauntings are frequently outlined as connections between our existence and substitute domains. The investigation of the obscure and the chance of correspondence with extraordinary elements has filled famous premium in substitute real factors.

Also, the domain of quantum physical science has brought the idea of equal universes into the area of logical request. Quantum mechanics, a crucial hypothesis in material science, recommends that particles can exist in numerous states at the same time until they are noticed. This idea brings about the possibility of the multiverse, where endless equal universes might exist, each with its own arrangement of actual regulations and constants.

The idea of the multiverse challenges the customary perspective on the universe as a particular, deterministic substance. All things being equal, it opens up the likelihood that there might be limitless varieties of the real world, going from those that intently look like our own to those where the laws of material science are completely unique. This thought has significant ramifications for how we might interpret the universe and the idea of the real world.

In the domain of contemporary sci-fi, the idea of substitute real factors keeps on being a rich wellspring of motivation. Creators like Philip K. Dick, in his book "The Man in the High Palace," and Michael Moorcock, in his "Timeless Hero" series, have made mind boggling stories that investigate the results of various verifiable results and the presence of different real factors. These works challenge perusers to examine the repercussions of different ways and the complexities of reality itself.

Equal universes have additionally advanced into the domain of mainstream society and amusement. TV series like "A Twilight Zone" and "Periphery" have dug into substitute real factors, offering watchers spellbinding stories that obscure the limits between the standard and the phenomenal. These accounts challenge our view of the real world and urge us to think about the possible presence of equal universes.

The idea of substitute real factors has found an unmistakable spot in computer games, where players can submerge themselves in virtual universes that exist together with our own world. Games like "The Legend of Zelda" and "Bioshock" make complicated, substitute real factors that permit players to investigate new aspects and potential outcomes. The intelligent idea of computer games gives a one of a kind stage to encountering and collaborating with equal universes.

The charm of equal universes stretches out past simple idealism and diversion. It takes advantage of the firmly established human interest in the obscure and the unfamiliar. It mixes our longing to wander past the limits of our ongoing information and to look for replies to the most significant inquiries regarding presence. Equal universes offer an enticing look into the limitless potential outcomes that might exist past our ongoing comprehension of the real world.

Besides, equal universes give a novel point of view on the outcomes of human decisions and activities. The idea that our choices in a single world could have expansive impacts in one more provokes us to think about the moral and moral elements of our decisions. It urges us to consider the interconnectedness of all life and the expected effect of our choices on the amazing woven artwork of presence.

Equal universes likewise offer a fruitful ground for investigating the idea of personality. In the event that there are endless forms of ourselves in equal universes, each with various encounters and results, what's the significance here to be "us"? Could it be said that we are characterized by our decisions, our conditions, or our innate characteristics? These inquiries challenge how we might interpret self as well as welcome us to consider the idea of through and through freedom and determinism.

In the domain of sci-fi, the idea of equal universes has been bridled to investigate the moral ramifications of cutting edge innovation, for example, equal universe travel or the making of fake real factors. These stories frequently act as wake up calls, advance notice us about the expected outcomes of messing with the limits of the real world. They help us to remember the requirement for mindful and moral utilization of innovation, particularly with regards to how we might interpret equal universes.

Equal universes are not restricted to the domain of sci-fi or reasoning; they have additionally tracked down their direction into different otherworldly and supernatural practices.

Numerous conviction frameworks incorporate the possibility of extraordinary domains or planes of presence. These domains are frequently viewed as where the spirit might pursue demise or where otherworldly creatures live. Now and again, people try to associate with these equal universes through reflection, custom, or other profound practices.

The idea of equal universes has additionally gotten some forward momentum with regards to quantum cognizance and the investigation of modified conditions of mindfulness. A few specialists and logicians propose that our impression of the truth isn't bound to a solitary, fixed aspect however can be modified and extended to incorporate different domains of cognizance. This point of view brings up issues about the idea of human discernment and the limits of how we might interpret reality.

1.3 The allure and fascination of parallel worlds

Equal universes, substitute real factors, or different aspects have held a strong and persevering through interest for mankind. This idea rises above time and culture, spellbinding the human creative mind across civic establishments and periods. The appeal of equal universes lies in their capability to open new points of view on the real world, offering the enticing possibility of investigating the huge obscure that exists past the limits of our ongoing comprehension. This interest can be followed through history, writing, reasoning, and contemporary sci-fi, uncovering the significant effect and getting through appeal of equal universes.

From the beginning of time, the idea of substitute real factors has been entwined with the texture of human culture. In antiquated legends, we find accounts of extraordinary domains possessed by divine beings, spirits, or heavenly creatures. These fantasies gave clarifications to the secrets of life, passing, and the hereafter. They offered bits of knowledge into the human condition and the idea of presence itself. In Greek folklore, for instance, the hidden world, controlled by Gehenna, was a particular substitute reality that housed the spirits of the departed. This fantasy filled in as a structure for understanding the change starting with one reality then onto the next, giving comfort and importance to the secrets of mortality.

Essentially, the Hindu conviction framework integrates the possibility of different domains or Lokas that exist close by our reality. Each Loka has its own remarkable qualities and occupants, mirroring a rich social and otherworldly practice that recognizes the presence of substitute real factors. Norse cosmology portrayed an intricate arrangement of domains, including Midgard (the human world) and Asgard (the domain of the divine beings). The confidence in these equal universes was necessary to Norse folklore and affected the Viking perspective. In old Egypt, the excursion to the great beyond was a focal part of strict conviction. Egyptians had confidence in an equal reality where the spirit would be judged, and, whenever viewed as commendable, would proceed to an everlasting presence within the sight of the divine beings. The idea of an equal domain of presence past death was a principal part of Egyptian culture, giving comfort and confirmation despite mortality.

The idea of equal universes has likewise flourished in the domain of writing and workmanship, where it has permitted social orders to investigate the limits of human creative mind. Abstract works have frequently worked as both amusement and psychological studies, testing the shows of the real world and welcoming perusers to consider the presence of different aspects. Lewis Carroll's "Alice's Undertakings in Wonderland" takes perusers on an unconventional excursion into a fantastical world that resists the laws of physical science and rationale. The account welcomes perusers to consider the constraints of the real world and the thought that substitute aspects could exist close by our own.

In "The Wizard of Oz" by L. Straightforward Baum, perusers are moved to the Place where there is Oz, a spot that coincides with the everyday world except is loaded up with supernatural animals and captivating undertakings. Baum's inventive world enthralled the creative mind of perusers and established the groundwork for a progression of equal world stories. These early works in writing tested customary ideas of the real world and broadened the limits of human creative mind.

The idea of substitute real factors has likewise influenced the domain of philosophical idea. Friedrich Nietzsche presented the thought of the "everlasting repeat," proposing that each occasion in the universe repeats limitlessly in endless equal universes. This idea brings up issues about the idea of presence, choice, and the certainty of human activities. Nietzsche's thoughts tested ordinary philosophical idea and supported examination of the expected presence of equal real factors.

As history advanced, the idea of substitute real factors proceeded to develop and adjust to the evolving times. The nineteenth and twentieth hundreds of years saw a flood in sci-fi writing and speculative fiction, which frequently investigated the subject of equal universes. Creators like H.G. Wells, with his book "The Conflict of the Universes," and Jules Verne, with "Excursion to the Focal point of the Earth," acquainted perusers with substitute aspects and universes concealed underneath the outer layer of the Earth. These accounts spellbound perusers' minds, testing how they might interpret reality and the potential outcomes that might exist past the limits of our reality.

The interest with equal universes has additionally been interlaced with the cutting edge interest with the extraordinary and the paranormal. Ideas like apparitions, spirits, and hauntings are frequently outlined as cooperations between our world and substitute domains. The investigation of the obscure and the chance of correspondence with supernatural elements has energized famous premium in substitute real factors, as individuals try to comprehend the secretive and the unexplained.

In addition, the domain of quantum material science has brought the idea of equal universes into the space of logical request. Quantum mechanics, a fundamental hypothesis in physical science, proposes that particles can exist in various states at the same time until they are noticed. This idea leads to the possibility of the multiverse, where innumerable equal universes might exist, each with its own arrangement of actual regulations and constants. The idea of the multiverse challenges the customary perspective on the universe as a particular, deterministic element. All things being equal, it opens up the likelihood that there might be endless varieties of the real world, going from those that intently look like our own to those where the laws of material science are altogether unique.

The idea of the multiverse has significant ramifications for how we might interpret the universe and the idea of the real world. It challenges our view of the universe and prompts us to consider the boundlessness and variety of the multiverse. This change in context challenges the regular perspective on the real world and welcomes us to think about the presence of equal universes past our ongoing comprehension.

In the domain of contemporary sci-fi, the idea of substitute real factors keeps on being a rich wellspring of motivation. Creators like Philip K. Dick, in his book "The Man in the High Palace," and Michael Moorcock, in his "Everlasting Hero" series, have created perplexing accounts that investigate the results of various authentic results and the presence of numerous real factors. These works challenge perusers to think about the repercussions of unique ways and the complexities of reality itself. Sci-fi, in this sense, fills in as a mirror to our own reality, expressing viewpoint inciting situations and welcoming us to ponder the ramifications of our decisions.

Equal universes have likewise advanced into the domain of mainstream society and diversion. TV series like "A Twilight Zone" and "Periphery" have dug into substitute real factors, offering watchers enrapturing stories that obscure the limits between the standard and the remarkable. These stories challenge our impression of the real world and urge us to think about the likely presence of equal universes.

The idea of substitute real factors has found a conspicuous spot in computer games, where players can drench themselves in virtual universes that exist together with our own world. Games like "The Legend of Zelda" and "Bioshock" make multifaceted, substitute real factors that permit players to investigate new aspects and potential outcomes. The intelligent idea of computer games gives an extraordinary stage to encountering and communicating with equal universes. Players can pursue decisions that impact the result of the game, offering a feeling of organization and commitment with the substitute reality.

The appeal of equal universes reaches out past simple idealism and amusement. It takes advantage of the well established human interest in the obscure and the strange.

It blends our craving to wander past the limits of our ongoing information and to look for replies to the most significant inquiries concerning presence. Equal universes offer a tempting look into the limitless conceivable outcomes that might exist past our ongoing comprehension of the real world.

Besides, equal universes give an interesting viewpoint on the outcomes of human decisions and activities. The thought that our choices in a single world could have broad impacts in one more moves us to think about the moral and moral elements of our decisions. It urges us to ponder the interconnectedness of all life and the likely effect of our choices on the excellent embroidery of presence.

Equal universes likewise offer a rich ground for investigating the idea of personality. Assuming that there are endless adaptations of ourselves in equal universes, each with various encounters and results, what's the significance here to be "us"? Is it true or not that we are characterized by our decisions, our conditions, or our intrinsic characteristics? These inquiries challenge how we might interpret self as well as welcome us to contemplate the idea of unrestrained choice and determinism. The investigation of personality in equal universes prompts us to think about the complexities of singularity and the elements that shape our healthy identity.

In the domain of sci-fi, the idea of equal universes has been tackled to investigate the moral ramifications of trend setting innovation, for example, equal universe travel or the production of counterfeit real factors. These stories frequently act as wake up calls, advance notice us about the possible results of altering the limits of the real world. They help us to remember the requirement for dependable and moral utilization of innovation, particularly with regards to how we might interpret equal universes.

Equal universes are not restricted to the domain of sci-fi or reasoning; they have likewise tracked down their direction into different otherworldly and supernatural practices. Numerous conviction frameworks incorporate the possibility of extraordinary domains or planes of presence.

Chapter 2

Parallel Worlds in Literature

Writing, as one of the most remarkable types of human articulation, has for quite some time been a jungle gym for investigating the idea of equal universes. Inside the pages of books, brief tales, and incredible sonnets, writers have made substitute real factors that enamor the creative mind, challenge regular ideas of the real world, and welcome perusers to contemplate the boundless potential outcomes that might exist past our own reality. The topic of equal universes in writing has a rich history that rises above time and culture, molding both the narratives we tell and our comprehension of the idea of the real world.

The interest with equal universes in writing is definitely not a new peculiarity yet has profound verifiable roots. Old legends and legendary stories from different societies frequently included domains that coincided with our own, offering looks into substitute real factors. For example, in Greek folklore, the hidden world, governed by Abbadon, was an equal world that filled in as the house of the departed. This mythic domain gave a system to understanding the change from life to death, offering a story structure that made sense of the secrets of mortality.

Equal universes found articulation in the Hindu conviction framework, which consolidates the idea of numerous domains or Lokas existing close by our reality. Each Loka has its own exceptional qualities and occupants, mirroring a rich social and profound practice that recognizes the presence of substitute real factors. These equal universes are not only different domains but rather indispensable parts of a mind boggling cosmology that shapes the Hindu perspective.

In Norse folklore, the idea of equal universes was profoundly imbued. The Norse universe included Midgard (the human world) and Asgard (the domain of the divine beings), alongside different domains like Jotunheim (the domain of goliaths) and Svartalfheim (the domain of dim mythical people). These domains coincided and connected, affecting the activities and destinies of the two humans and divine beings. The confidence in these equal universes was a key part of Norse folklore and significantly affected the Viking comprehension of the world.

Equal universes likewise assumed a focal part in old Egyptian convictions. The excursion to eternity was a critical part of Egyptian religion, and the idea of an equal world past death was essential to their way of life. In this substitute reality, the spirit would be judged, and, whenever saw as commendable, would proceed to an everlasting presence within the sight of the divine beings. The possibility of an equal domain of presence past death was a basic component of Egyptian culture, giving comfort and motivation despite mortality.

As writing created throughout the long term, the subject of equal universes proceeded to develop and adjust to changing social and scholarly scenes. Equal universes tracked down their direction into epic sonnets, for example, Dante Alighieri's "The Heavenly Parody," which takes perusers on an excursion through some serious hardship, Limbo, and Heaven. Dante's work investigates the possibility of numerous domains of presence and fills in as a figurative portrayal of the spirit's excursion towards God, with every domain addressing various parts of the human experience.

Equal universes likewise spread the word about their presence in archaic sentiments and stories of gallantry. Arthurian legends, for instance, frequently highlighted the idea of charmed woods, legendary islands, and powerful domains. These accounts extended the limits of reality by acquainting perusers with equal universes where enchantment and experience ruled. The idea of powerful domains gave fruitful ground to investigating the subjects of valor, fate, and the extraordinary.

In the Renaissance, the subject of equal universes went through a change, driven by the extension of information, investigation, and logical request. Crafted by writers like Sir Thomas More, with his book "Perfect world," acquainted perusers with a glorified equal reality where cultural standards were upset to incite reflection on the weaknesses of contemporary society. More's work established the groundwork for a class of writing known as idealistic fiction, which investigates the idea of an other reality where social and political frameworks vary from those in the writer's reality.

Equal universes got further consideration during the Edification, a period set apart by a developing interest in reason, judiciousness, and logical investigation. Scholars and thinkers of this period started to examine the presence of substitute real factors in a more precise and speculative way. Voltaire's sarcastic novella "Micromégas" imagined life on different planets, displaying the possibility of shrewd creatures possessing equal universes in the tremendous universe.

In the nineteenth hundred years, equal universes tracked down a conspicuous spot in the arising sort of sci-fi. Creators like H.G. Wells, Jules Verne, and Mary Shelley utilized the idea of equal universes to create inventive and provocative accounts. Wells' "The Conflict of the Universes" portrayed an other reality where Earth is attacked by Martians, moving perusers to think about the results of an experience with extraterrestrial creatures. Verne's "Excursion to the Focal point of the Earth" acquainted perusers with an underground world, proposing that secret domains could exist underneath the outer layer of our planet.

Equal universes likewise showed up in progress of Edgar Allan Poe, who dove into the domain of the extraordinary and the unexplored world. His brief tale "The Obvious Heart" investigates the limits of reality as the storyteller's insight turns out to be progressively contorted, obscuring the line between the normal and the remarkable.

Poe's accounts frequently provoked perusers to think about the delicacy of human discernment and the expected presence of substitute real factors inside the human psyche.

Perhaps of the most renowned and getting through work that investigates the topic of equal universes is Lewis Carroll's "Alice's Experiences in Wonderland." In this eccentric and dreamlike story, Alice coincidentally finds a fantastical reality where rationale and reason are supplanted by ludicrousness and caprice. The story welcomes perusers to consider the constraints of the real world and the thought that substitute aspects could exist close by our own. Carroll's work has kept on dazzling perusers, everything being equal, testing how they might interpret reality and welcoming them to leave on an inventive excursion down the deep, dark hole.

Essentially, L. Plain Baum's "The Wizard of Oz" acquainted perusers with the Place that is known for Oz, a spot that coincides with the everyday world except is loaded up with mysterious animals and captivating undertakings. Baum's creative world dazzled the creative mind of perusers and established the groundwork for a progression of equal world stories, proceeding with the practice of investigating substitute real factors in writing.

Equal universes have likewise been entwined with the topics of character and duality in writing. Robert Louis Stevenson's novella "Abnormal Instance of Dr. Jekyll and Mr. Hyde" presents a person who encapsulates the duality of human instinct, with Dr. Jekyll and Mr. Hyde addressing two particular characters existing inside a similar person. The story brings up issues about the limits of character and the potential for substitute personas to rise up out of inside.

In the domain of philosophical writing, Friedrich Nietzsche presented the idea of the "everlasting repeat," recommending that each occasion in the universe repeats a boundless number of times. This thought difficulties the customary comprehension of time and presence, empowering perusers to mull over the idea of the real world and the results of everlasting redundancy. Nietzsche's psychological test welcomes perusers to consider the presence of equal universes where situation transpire in vast cycles.

Equal universes have likewise advanced into contemporary writing, where writers keep on investigating the idea with new points of view and inventive accounts. Philip K. Dick, known for his brain twisting sci-fi, expressed "The Man in the High Palace," an original that envisions a substitute reality wherein the Pivot powers won The Second Great War. Dick's work moves perusers to mull over the outcomes of verifiable occasions and the complex interaction of substitute narratives.

Creators like Michael Moorcock, in his "Everlasting Hero" series, have made complex accounts that investigate the presence of various real factors and the timeless battle between vast powers. Moorcock's work moves perusers to consider the inter-connectedness of equal universes and the effect of individual decisions on the destiny of the multiverse.

Equal universes additionally track down their place in youthful grown-up and dream writing, where writers like Philip Pullman, with his "His Dim Materials" series, acquaint perusers with equal aspects and the idea of daemons, mirroring the intricacy of human instinct and the investigation of powerful domains. The charm of equal universes in writing rises above age and type, interesting to perusers of all foundations and interests.

The interest with equal universes in writing goes past simple idealism and amuse-ment. It takes advantage of the human interest in the obscure and the unknown. It mixes the longing to wander past the limits of our ongoing information and to look for replies to the most significant inquiries regarding presence. Equal universes offer a tempting look into the endless conceivable outcomes that might exist past our on-going comprehension of the real world.

Besides, equal universes in writing act as a mirror to our own reality, permitting us to investigate complex subjects and inquiries regarding character, decision, and the idea of the real world. The idea of substitute real factors provokes perusers to ponder the moral and moral elements of their decisions and activities. It urges us to think about the interconnectedness of all life and the likely effect of our choices on the fabulous woven artwork of presence.

2.1 Literary works that explore parallel worlds

The topic of equal universes, substitute real factors, or different aspects has been an enduring and enamoring subject in writing, offering a material for writers to investi-gate the boundless limits of human creative mind. These works of fiction length a large number of classifications and styles, from old fantasies to contemporary sci-fi, and they have kept on dazzling perusers with their interesting stories. This investigation of artistic works that dig into equal universes uncovers the profundity and variety of the idea's presence in writing and its significant effect on the human comprehension of the real world.

Folklore and Incredible stories:

Equal universes have a well established presence in the fantasies and legendary stories of different societies. In Greek folklore, the idea of the hidden world, controlled by Abbadon, was an equal existence where the spirits of the departed lived. This mythic domain gave a clarification to the progress from life to death, offering experi-ences into the human condition and the secrets of mortality. Additionally, in Hindu conviction frameworks, numerous Lokas or domains exist together with our reality, each with its one of a kind qualities and occupants. These domains are vital to the Hindu cosmology, mirroring the many-sided embroidered artwork of equal universes in antiquated Indian culture.

Norse folklore, with its rich pantheon of divine beings and domains, acquainted perusers with equal universes that coincided with the human domain. The domains of Midgard, Asgard, Jotunheim, and Svartalfheim offered a perplexing cosmology where divine beings, monsters, and different creatures interfaced. This perspective significantly affected the Viking comprehension of the world, featuring the interconnectedness of equal real factors.

Renaissance and Idealistic Fiction:

The Renaissance time frame saw a resurgence of interest in the idea of equal universes, driven by scholarly interest and investigation. Sir Thomas More's "Ideal world," distributed in 1516, is a fundamental work in the class of idealistic fiction. It acquainted perusers with an admired equal reality where cultural standards were rearranged to incite reflection on the weaknesses of contemporary society. More's work established the groundwork for a subgenre of writing that imagines substitute real factors intended to challenge and study the common standards of the writer's time.

The Illumination and Philosophical Hypothesis:

The Illumination period denoted a period of reason, judiciousness, and logical request, during which creators started to mull over the presence of substitute real factors all the more methodicallly and hypothetically. Voltaire's ironical novella "Micromégas," distributed in 1752, envisions clever creatures from different planets, widening the idea of equal universes. The story moves perusers to think about extraterrestrial life and the ramifications of such experiences.

Sci-fi and nineteenth Century Writing:

The nineteenth century saw a flood in sci-fi and speculative writing, where the subject of equal universes acquired further noticeable quality. Creators like H.G. Wells, Jules Verne, and Mary Shelley utilized the idea of substitute real factors to make creative accounts. Wells' "The Conflict of the Universes" portrays an other reality where Earth is attacked by Martians, inciting perusers to think about the results of contact with extraterrestrial creatures. Jules Verne's "Excursion to the Focal point of the Earth" takes perusers on an underground experience, recommending stowed away domains underneath the World's surface. Mary Shelley's "Frankenstein" investigates the limits of life and passing, obscuring the lines among science and the extraordinary, and acquainting perusers with moral issues chasing after logical headway.

Oddity and the Oblivious Psyche:

In the twentieth 100 years, the surrealist development in writing and craftsmanship embraced the idea of equal universes for the purpose of investigating the psyche and the limits of the real world. Surrealist creators, like André Breton and Salvador Dali, made works that tested customary thoughts of time, space, and character. Their works frequently highlighted fanciful situations and strange scenes, welcoming perusers to think about the perplexing and unreasonable nature of the human psyche.

Alice's Undertakings in Wonderland:

Lewis Carroll's "Alice's Undertakings in Wonderland" (1865) remains as quite possibly of the most famous work that investigate the idea of equal universes. In this capricious and dreamlike story, Alice coincidentally finds a fantastical existence where rationale and reason are supplanted by craziness and eccentricity.

The story welcomes perusers to consider the constraints of the real world and the idea that substitute aspects could exist close by our own. Carroll's work has kept on dazzling perusers, everything being equal, testing how they might interpret reality and welcoming them to set out on an inventive excursion down the deep, dark hole.

The Wizard of Oz:

L. Blunt Baum's "The Wizard of Oz" (1900) acquainted perusers with the Place where there is Oz, a spot that coincides with the everyday world except is loaded up with otherworldly animals and charming undertakings. Baum's creative world enamored the creative mind of perusers and established the groundwork for a progression of equal world stories, proceeding with the practice of investigating substitute real factors in writing.

Personality and Duality:

The subject of character and duality is a repetitive theme in writing that investigates equal universes. Robert Louis Stevenson's novella "Unusual Instance of Dr. Jekyll and Mr. Hyde" (1886) presents a person who encapsulates the duality of human instinct, with Dr. Jekyll and Mr. Hyde addressing two particular characters existing inside a similar person. The story brings up issues about the limits of personality and the potential for substitute personas to rise out of inside.

Sci-fi and Substitute Narratives:

In the domain of sci-fi, equal universes have been outfit to investigate the results of various authentic results and the presence of different real factors. Philip K. Dick's "The Man in the High Palace" (1962) imagines a substitute reality where the Hub powers won The Second Great War. Dick's work provokes perusers to think about the results of authentic occasions and the mind boggling transaction of substitute chronicles.

The Multiverse and Contemporary Sci-fi:

Contemporary sci-fi writing has embraced the idea of the multiverse, where various equal universes exist, each with its extraordinary arrangement of actual regulations and constants. Creators like Michael Moorcock, in his "Everlasting Hero" series, have made perplexing stories that investigate the presence of various real factors and the timeless battle between enormous powers. Moorcock's work provokes perusers to consider the interconnectedness of equal universes and the effect of individual decisions on the destiny of the multiverse.

Youthful Grown-up and Dream Writing:

Equal universes have likewise tracked down an unmistakable spot in youthful grown-up and dream writing. Philip Pullman's "His Dim Materials" series acquaints perusers with equal aspects and the idea of daemons, mirroring the intricacy of human instinct and the investigation of powerful domains. These works resound with a different crowd and keep on dazzling perusers with their creative stories.

Intelligent Fiction and Computer games:

Equal universes have not been restricted to the pages of books however have additionally advanced into different types of media. Computer games, specifically, have embraced the idea of substitute real factors, permitting players to drench themselves in virtual universes that coincide with our own world. Games like "The Legend of Zelda" and "Bioshock" make multifaceted, substitute real factors that empower players to investigate new aspects and potential outcomes. The intelligent idea of computer games gives an extraordinary stage to encountering and interfacing with equal universes.

Equal Universes in Contemporary Mainstream society:

Lately, the idea of equal universes has advanced into mainstream society and amusement in different structures, including TV series, motion pictures, and computer generated reality encounters. These advancements empower crowds to submerge themselves in equal universes and investigate the boundless conceivable outcomes they offer. As innovation keeps on propelling, the limit between the virtual and the genuine foggy spots, and the investigation of substitute real factors turns out to be more available and enthralling.

The interest with equal universes in writing rises above age, classification, and social limits. These artistic works tap into the well established human interest in the obscure and the unknown, welcoming perusers to wander past the limits of their ongoing information and look for replies to the most significant inquiries regarding presence. Equal universes act as a mirror to our own world, permitting us to investigate complex subjects and inquiries regarding character, decision, and the idea of the real world.

The idea of substitute real factors provokes perusers to ponder the moral and moral components of their decisions and activities. It urges us to think about the interconnectedness of all life and the likely effect of our choices on the fantastic embroidered artwork of presence. Equal universes offer a rich ground for investigating the idea of personality, as characters in writing frequently wrestle with their numerous selves across various aspects. The possibility that people might exist in different structures in equal universes prompts perusers to consider the idea of self, the effect of decisions, and the mission for credibility.

Equal universes in writing likewise act as a strong stage for social discourse and social scrutinize. They offer writers the chance to envision substitute social orders, frameworks, and standards, moving perusers to consider the potential outcomes and results of various approaches to coordinating human life. From the perspective of equal universes, creators can feature the qualities and shortcomings of their own general public while offering a dream of what could be.

2.2 Analysis of key texts and their impact

The idea of equal universes has assumed a significant and persevering through part in writing, giving ripe ground to investigating the limits of human creative mind, testing ordinary thoughts of the real world, and provoking perusers to ponder the secrets of presence. Over the course of writing, a few key texts have made a permanent imprint, forming the manner in which we contemplate equal universes and their significant effect on how we might interpret the human condition. This examination digs into a portion of these urgent texts, their topics, and the enduring impact they have had on writing and culture.

"Alice's Undertakings in Wonderland" by Lewis Carroll (1865):

Lewis Carroll's "Alice's Undertakings in Wonderland" remains as a fundamental work in the investigation of equal universes. Through the unconventional story of Alice, who tumbles down a deep, dark hole into a fantastical domain, Carroll provokes perusers to reexamine the limits of the real world. Wonderland is where rationale and reason are superseded by craziness and eccentricity. The effect of this text stretches out past its inventive narrating; it has turned into a persevering through social standard that welcomes perusers, everything being equal, to leave on a creative excursion.

Carroll's work acquaints perusers with the idea of an equal world that exists together with the common, where the laws of physical science and rationale are not restricting. This other reality fills in as a mirror to our own reality, stressing the erratic and frequently silly nature of the standards that oversee regular daily existence. The characters and scenes of Wonderland, for example, the Cheshire Feline and the Sovereign of Hearts, have become famous figures in writing and mainstream society.

Also, "Alice's Undertakings in Wonderland" brings up philosophical issues about personality and the idea of the real world. Alice experiences different adaptations of herself as well as other people in Wonderland, testing customary ideas of self and personality. The text prompts perusers to think about the ease of personality and the effect of one's environmental factors on one's healthy identity.

The enduring effect of Carroll's work is clear in its proceeded with fame, various variations in different media, and its impact on resulting creators and specialists. The text has roused innumerable works of writing, film, and workmanship that investigate the idea of equal universes and the obscuring of limits among the real world and creative mind.

"The Wizard of Oz" by L. Straight to the point Baum (1900):

L. Straight to the point Baum's "The Wizard of Oz" acquaints perusers with the Place that is known for Oz, a spot that coincides with the commonplace world yet is loaded up with mysterious animals and charming experiences.

Baum's work has left a getting through inheritance, enthralling perusers with its innovative narrating and its investigation of equal universes.

"The Wizard of Oz" investigates subjects of self-revelation, boldness, and the mission for home. The hero, Dorothy, sets out on an excursion through Oz, where she experiences a different cast of characters and faces various difficulties. The Place where there is Oz fills in as an equal world that challenges' comprehension Dorothy might interpret reality and prompts her to investigate the profundities of her own personality.

The effect of "The Wizard of Oz" reaches out past the pages of the book. The story's transformation into the notorious 1939 film featuring Judy Wreath set its place in mainstream society. The persevering through allure of Oz has roused innumerable transformations, side projects, and reevaluations, exhibiting the persevering through interest with the idea of equal universes and the force of narrating to move perusers and crowds to new domains.

"Unusual Instance of Dr. Jekyll and Mr. Hyde" by Robert Louis Stevenson (1886):

Robert Louis Stevenson's novella "Unusual Instance of Dr. Jekyll and Mr. Hyde" dives into the subject of personality and duality, a repetitive theme in writing that investigates equal universes inside oneself. The text acquaints perusers with Dr. Jekyll, a regarded doctor, and his change self image, Mr. Hyde, a pernicious and flippant person. The story brings up issues about the limits of personality and the potential for substitute personas to rise up out of inside.

Stevenson's work is a mental investigation of the human mind and the double idea of mankind. It prompts perusers to consider the hazier parts of human instinct and the results of stifling one's internal evil presences. The idea of equal universes inside a solitary individual difficulties conventional thoughts of self and character.

"Dr. Jekyll and Mr. Hyde" lastingly affects writing and mainstream society. It has turned into a reference point for conversations of human brain science, the duality of human instinct, and the outcomes of moral and moral decisions. The novella's getting through impact is a demonstration of its capacity to reverberate with perusers and incite reflection on the intricacies of the human condition.

"The Man in the High Palace" by Philip K. Dick (1962):

Philip K. Dick's "The Man in the High Palace" is a sci-fi novel that imagines an other reality where the Hub powers won The Second Great War, bringing about a separated US. The novel is an investigation of substitute chronicles and their effect on individual and aggregate fates.

"The Man in the High Palace" moves perusers to think about the outcomes of verifiable occasions and the multifaceted exchange of substitute accounts. The text brings up issues about the delicacy of verifiable results and the potential for disparate real factors in view of vital minutes previously. It fills in as a provocative investigation of the idea of equal universes and the possibility that various decisions can prompt immeasurably various results.

The effect of Philip K. Dick's work stretches out to the domain of sci-fi and substitute history writing. It has motivated ensuing creators to investigate comparable subjects, frequently with an emphasis on the moral and moral components of verifiable decisions. The clever's transformation into a well known TV series has additionally solidified its spot in the social cognizance, welcoming watchers to think about the likely results of option verifiable directions.

"His Dim Materials" series by Philip Pullman (1995-2000):

Philip Pullman's "His Dim Materials" set of three, which incorporates "Aurora Borealis" (otherwise called "The Brilliant Compass"), "The Unpretentious Blade," and "The Golden Spyglass," is a youthful grown-up and dream series that investigates equal aspects and the idea of daemons. The series essentially affects writing, igniting conversations about the idea of awareness and the interconnectedness of universes.

Pullman's work acquaints perusers with equal aspects and daemons, which are actual signs of an individual's internal identity. The idea of equal universes in the series brings up issues about the idea of awareness and the likely presence of different aspects past our own. It prompts perusers to consider the intricacies of human instinct and the possibility that people might exist in various structures across various real factors.

The "His Dull Materials" series significantly affects the youthful grown-up and dream classes. Its investigation of equal universes, moral quandaries, and the idea of presence has reverberated with perusers, everything being equal. The series has motivated philosophical conversations and has been adjusted into different media, including a TV series, further solidifying its status as a socially critical work.

"Initiation" (Movie) coordinated by Christopher Nolan (2010):

While not a scholarly text, Christopher Nolan's film "Beginning" essentially affects the investigation of equal universes in mainstream society. The film follows a gathering of people who enter the fantasies of others to impact their considerations and activities. The idea of dream layers inside dream layers presents equal real factors inside the brain.

"Beginning" moves watchers to mull over the limits of the real world and the pliability of the human brain. The film obscures the lines among dreams and reality, inciting conversations about the idea of discernment and the likely presence of equal universes inside the inner mind.

The effect of "Commencement" stretches out to the domain of film and mainstream society. It has turned into a reference point for conversations of dreams, reality, and the force of the human psyche. The film's imaginative account construction and investigation of equal universes have made an enduring imprint on contemporary narrating and filmmaking.

"Dim" (television Series) made by Baran bo Odar and Jantje Friese (2017-2020):

The German TV series "Dim" is a great representation of how the investigation of equal universes and time travel can be convincing and interesting. The series winds around a complicated story that includes different ages and interconnected timetables. It provokes watchers to consider the ramifications of time travel and the presence of equal real factors.

"Dull" dives into topics of determinism, through and through freedom, and the results of one's activities across various time spans. The series prompts watchers to ponder the many-sided interaction of time, causality, and the potential for equal universes to coincide inside a solitary course of events.

The effect of "Dull" stretches out to the domain of TV and sci-fi narrating. The series has been lauded for its multifaceted narrating and its capacity to draw in watchers in complex accounts. It fills in to act as an illustration of how the idea of equal universes can be investigated in a contemporary and refined way, testing the limits of conventional narrating.

"The Long Earth" series by Terry Pratchett and Stephen Baxter (2012-2016):

Terry Pratchett and Stephen Baxter's "The Long Earth" series is a work of speculative fiction that investigates the presence of a large number of equal Earths, each open through a basic gadget. The series brings up issues about the idea of mankind, investigation, and the results of limitless conceivable outcomes.

2.3 How authors use parallel worlds to convey themes and ideas

The idea of equal universes, substitute real factors, and different aspects in writing fills in as a rich and flexible material for writers to convey a large number of subjects and thoughts. Through the investigation of these different domains, creators can dive into philosophical requests, social analysis, and the intricacies of human life. This examination digs into how creators bridle the idea of equal universes to convey subjects and thoughts, featuring the profundity and variety of narrating conceivable outcomes.

Reflections on The real world and Insight:

One of the essential ways writers utilize equal universes is to challenge the's comprehension peruser might interpret reality and discernment. By giving substitute aspects that coincide the ordinary world, writers incite perusers to scrutinize the dependability of their own existence. They brief us to think about how conceivable it is that there are numerous layers of presence past what is quickly evident.

In Lewis Carroll's "Alice's Undertakings in Wonderland," the fantastical universe of Wonderland upsets regular rationale and resists the laws of physical science. By encountering this equal reality through Alice's viewpoint, perusers are urged to scrutinize the restrictions of their own insight and to embrace the possibility that reality can be abstract and consistently moving. Carroll's work features the erratic idea of the guidelines that oversee our lives, welcoming us to ponder the flexibility of insight and the presence of various layers of the real world.

Furthermore, creators like Philip K. Dick, in works like "The Man in the High Palace," challenge perusers to stand up to the delicacy of verifiable reality. The idea of substitute accounts in this clever powers us to wrestle with the possibility that set of experiences can be reworked in view of various decisions or occasions. It urges perusers to scrutinize the steadiness of verifiable insights and to perceive the abstract idea of authentic stories.

Personality and the Assortment of Self:

Equal universes in writing regularly act as a scenery for investigating the subject of character. Creators frequently present characters who should explore different variants of themselves across various aspects. This investigation brings up issues about the idea of self and the effect of decisions on one's character.

Robert Louis Stevenson's "Weird Instance of Dr. Jekyll and Mr. Hyde" typifies this subject, with the hero, Dr. Jekyll, and his pernicious modify self image, Mr. Hyde, addressing two unmistakable aspects of a similar person. The story challenges the customary idea of a brought together self and prompts perusers to think about the duality that exists inside all people. The idea of equal universes inside a solitary mind highlights that people might have different characters or personas, each competing for strength.

Essentially, Philip Pullman's "His Dull Materials" series presents the idea of daemons, actual signs of an individual's internal identity, in equal universes. This investigation mirrors the intricacy of human instinct and proposes that character isn't static however can show diversely in different aspects. Pullman's work urges perusers to consider the variety of self and the always advancing nature of character.

Moral and Moral Difficulties:

Equal universes in writing frequently act as a phase for moral and moral difficulties. Creators make situations in what characters should wrestle with significant decisions and their outcomes across various real factors. These issues brief perusers to think about the moral components of their own choices and activities.

In "The Man in the High Palace," Philip K. Dick's other history novel, characters stand up to the ethical ramifications of a reality where the Pivot powers arose triumphant in The Second Great War.

The original welcomes perusers to consider the outcomes of authentic occasions and the moral issues that emerge when confronted with the decisions made by people and social orders.

The investigation of moral and moral aspects reaches out to sci-fi works that dig into cutting edge innovation, for example, equal universe travel. Creators like H.G. Wells and Christopher Nolan, in "Commencement," present accounts that feature the expected results of altering the limits of the real world and the moral obligations that accompany such power. These works alert perusers about the requirement for capable and moral utilization of innovation, particularly with regards to how we might interpret equal universes.

Investigation of Cultural Standards and Frameworks:

Equal universes in writing offer writers a stage to investigate cultural standards, frameworks, and designs. By presenting substitute real factors, writers can introduce social orders that challenge the overarching standards of the writer's time, offering perusers a new viewpoint on friendly issues.

Sir Thomas More's "Perfect world," an essential work in the class of idealistic fiction, presents a glorified equal existence where cultural standards are modified to evaluate the deficiencies of contemporary society. More's work provokes perusers to reexamine the social frameworks and standards of their own time and to imagine elective approaches to arranging human life.

In like manner, Terry Pratchett and Stephen Baxter's "The Long Earth" series digs into topics of investigation, colonization, and cultural standards. The series investigates the moral and moral ramifications of limitless admittance to resemble universes and prompts perusers to consider the decisions and difficulties that emerge when stood up to with the immeasurability of the multiverse. It welcomes us to scrutinize the designs and frameworks that administer human collaboration and association.

Time, Causality, and Freedom of thought:

Equal universes frequently converge with the topics of time, causality, and unrestrained choice. Creators utilize these substitute aspects to investigate the outcomes of various decisions and the complexities of time travel.

The German TV series "Dull" is a perfect representation of how creators can utilize equal universes to dig into the intricacies of time and causality. The series winds around a story that includes various ages and interconnected courses of events, provoking watchers to consider the ramifications of time travel and the presence of equal real factors. It prompts us to ponder the exchange of time, causality, and the potential for equal universes to coincide inside a solitary course of events.

Christopher Nolan's "Origin" investigates the idea of dreams inside dreams, obscuring the lines between various layers of the real world. The film brings up issues about the idea of discernment and the flexibility of time inside dreams. It moves watchers to think about the ramifications of time control and the likely presence of equal universes inside the inner mind.

Investigation of Dread and the Unexplored world:

Equal universes can act as a vehicle for investigating dread, the obscure, and the human interest with the unfamiliar. By acquainting perusers with new aspects, creators can summon a feeling of miracle and fear.

H.P. Lovecraft's "The Fantasy Mission of Obscure Kadath" takes perusers on an excursion through a fantasy land loaded up with weird animals and eldritch scenes. Lovecraft's work takes advantage of the apprehension about the obscure and the feeling of amazement and fear that goes with the investigation of equal universes. It highlights that equal real factors can be both charming and unnerving.

Also, Lewis Carroll's "Alice's Experiences in Wonderland" and L. Candid Baum's "The Wizard of Oz" catch the feeling of marvel and experience that goes with the disclosure of equal universes. These works bring out the adventure of investigation and the expectation of experiencing the new. They help us to remember the human limit with regards to interest and the appeal of the unfamiliar.

Chapter 3

Quantum Mechanics and Many-Worlds

Quantum mechanics, a key hypothesis of material science, has been a subject of interest and debate since its commencement in the mid twentieth 100 years. It challenges our old style instincts about the way of behaving of issue and energy, offering a dumbfounding and frequently outlandish look into the infinitesimal domain of the universe. One of the most interesting translations of quantum mechanics is the Many-Universes speculation, which proposes a revolutionary reconsidering of the real world. In this investigation, we will dive profound into the complicated universe of quantum mechanics and the psyche twisting idea of Many-Universes, endeavoring to unwind the secrets that encompass this captivating field of study.

Quantum mechanics, usually alluded to as quantum material science or quantum hypothesis, is a part of physical science that gives a system to grasping the way of behaving of particles at the nuclear and subatomic level. It has its underlying foundations underway of mid twentieth century physicists like Max Planck, Albert Einstein, Niels Bohr, and Erwin Schrödinger. These splendid personalities set up for a transformation in how we might interpret the actual world. The foundation of quantum mechanics is the wave-molecule duality, which proposes that particles like electrons and photons can display both wave-like and molecule like way of behaving.

At the core of quantum mechanics is the Schrödinger condition, a key condition that depicts how the quantum condition of a framework develops after some time. This condition frames the reason for understanding the likelihood appropriation of particles in different quantum states. Dissimilar to old style material science, which gives exact determinism, quantum mechanics works in a probabilistic domain. This intrinsic eccentricism has brought about the absolute most confounding peculiarities in the field.

One of the most renowned parts of quantum mechanics is the Heisenberg Vulnerability Standard, planned by Werner Heisenberg in 1927. This standard declares that it is difficult to know the specific position and force of a molecule with full confidence at the same time. The more precisely we know one of these properties, the less precisely we can know the other. This vulnerability challenges our old style thought of a precision universe and presents a component of inborn irregularity into the texture of the real world.

One more baffling peculiarity in quantum mechanics is entrapment, broadly portrayed by Albert Einstein as "creepy activity a ways off." Snare happens when at least two particles become connected so that the condition of one molecule immediately impacts the condition of another, no matter what the distance that isolates them. This apparently non-nearby association has bewildered physicists and has been the subject of many analyses and discussions.

Quantum mechanics likewise presents the idea of superposition, which expresses that a quantum framework can exist in a mix of various states all the while. This implies that a molecule can be in various places or states without a moment's delay, until it is estimated or noticed. At the point when an estimation is made, the superposition "falls" into one of the potential results, with not entirely set in stone by the wave capability. This thought difficulties our old style instinct, as it recommends that particles can exist in a condition of equivocalness until they are noticed, so, all in all they expect a clear state.

The Copenhagen translation, formed by Niels Bohr and Werner Heisenberg, is one of the most well known and talked about understandings of quantum mechanics. As per this translation, the demonstration of estimation or perception is key to the breakdown of the quantum wave capability, deciding the result and driving the framework into one of the potential states. This understanding accentuates the job of the spectator and infers that the quantum world is innately questionable until estimated.

Be that as it may, the Copenhagen translation has brought up philosophical issues and discussions about the idea of the real world. It leaves the eyewitness as a central part of the cycle, prompting inquiries regarding the presence of an objective reality free of perception. This discussion has started the improvement of elective understandings, one of the most fascinating being the Many-Universes translation.

The Many-Universes understanding, first proposed by Hugh Everett III in quite a while, an extreme takeoff from the Copenhagen translation. As indicated by Many-Universes, there is no breakdown of the wave capability upon estimation. All things considered, each conceivable result of a quantum occasion happens, and every result branches into a different, non-conveying equal universe. In this understanding, the universe continually branches into a limitless number of equal real factors, each addressing an alternate result of each and every quantum occasion.

In a Many-Universes situation, if you somehow managed to flip a quantum coin, the universe would part into two branches — one where the coin lands heads up and another where it lands tails up. In another model, on the off chance that a molecule is in a superposition of two expresses, the universe bifurcates into two particular real factors, one for every conceivable condition of the molecule. This translation recommends that all potential results are acknowledged in equal universes, making a practically boundless cluster of existing together, non-connecting universes.

The Many-Universes understanding endeavors to determine the obvious mysteries and philosophical problems presented by quantum mechanics. It offers a total and deterministic depiction of quantum occasions, where all potential results are acknowledged in isolated parts of the real world. This translation eliminates the requirement for wave capability breakdown and gives a consistent clarification to the way of behaving of particles in superposition and trap.

One of the huge qualities of the Many-Universes understanding is its capacity to give a clear and inside reliable record of quantum peculiarities. Dissimilar to the Copenhagen translation, which conjures the strange idea of wave capability breakdown, Many-Universes sticks to the standards of unitary development and determinism. In this structure, the Schrödinger condition generally oversees the development of quantum frameworks, without the requirement for extra hypothesizes about the job of estimation.

Many-Universes likewise offers a wonderful answer for the estimation issue, an essential issue in quantum mechanics that concerns the change from a superposition of states to an unequivocal estimation result. In the Many-Universes understanding, this progress is consistent, as all potential results are acknowledged in particular parts of the real world. There is compelling reason need to summon extraordinary standards for the job of the eyewitness, as the onlooker is simply a piece of the general quantum framework.

Besides, Many-Universes gives a rich clarification to the peculiarity of quantum ensnarement. In this understanding, trapped particles in a superposition state exist in discrete parts of the real world, it are impeccably corresponded to guarantee that their properties. The clear non-territory of entrapment is settled, as the particles are presently not in a similar universe however exist in equal branches.

In spite of its hypothetical polish and allure, the Many-Universes understanding isn't without its faultfinders and difficulties. One of the essential reactions is the sheer luxury of placing a boundless number of equal universes. Pundits contend that this translation presents a pointless degree of intricacy and needs experimental proof to help the presence of these equal universes.

Also, the Many-Universes understanding has confronted philosophical complaints connected with the idea of individual character and the idea of likelihood. A few pundits contend that the expansion of equal universes brings up issues about how individual personality is protected as a singular pursues decisions in various parts of the real world. Others fight that the idea of likelihood becomes dangerous, as it is muddled the way in which probabilities are appointed across a boundless number of equal universes.

One more analysis of Many-Universes relates to its capacity to represent naturally visible items and traditional way of behaving. While the understanding is appropriate to make sense of the way of behaving of quantum particles, it turns out to be more difficult to legitimize how old style, ordinary articles, like seats and vehicles, rise up out of the quantum world.

Pundits contend that Many-Universes misses the mark on clear component for the development of traditional reality from the quantum domain.

The discussion over the Many-Universes translation keeps on being a subject of extreme conversation and examination inside the field of quantum mechanics. While it offers a rich and inside reliable structure, it stays a subject of hypothesis and understanding, as giving direct trial proof to the presence of equal universes is troublesome.

Lately, specialists have investigated the potential for trial of the Many-Universes speculation. Some have suggested that specific quantum tests could give circuitous proof to the presence of equal universes. Nonetheless, such trials are still in the domain of hypothetical hypothesis and have not yet yielded authoritative outcomes.

One more way to deal with examining the Many-Universes understanding is through the improvement of quantum PCs. These gadgets, which saddle the standards of quantum mechanics, can possibly play out specific estimations more productively than old style PCs. Some contend that the abilities of quantum PCs are demonstrative of the presence of equal universes, as these PCs exploit the quantum peculiarities on which Many-Universes is based.

As how we might interpret quantum mechanics extends, taking into account the philosophical ramifications of the Many-Universes interpretation is fundamental. This understanding difficulties our view of the real world and the job of perception in the quantum domain.

3.1 Introduction to quantum mechanics

Quantum mechanics is a central hypothesis in physical science that upset comprehension we might interpret the way of behaving of issue and energy at the littlest scales. A system depicts the properties and communications of particles and waves on the nuclear and subatomic level. This hypothesis, which arose in the mid twentieth hundred years, tested traditional material science, presenting ideas that were frequently strange and secretive. In this extensive prologue to quantum mechanics, we will investigate the crucial standards, key peculiarities, and authentic improvement of this momentous hypothesis.

The introduction of quantum mechanics can be followed back to the late nineteenth and mid twentieth hundreds of years when physicists were wrestling with peculiarities that traditional material science neglected to make sense of. One of the main difficulties was figuring out the way of behaving of light. Traditional material science regarded light as a nonstop wave, however tests like the photoelectric impact, saw by Albert Einstein in 1905, showed that light displayed molecule like properties. This peculiarity proposed that light could be quantized into discrete bundles of energy, called quanta.

In 1900, Max Planck acquainted the idea of quantization with make sense of the radiation produced by a hot item, like a blackbody radiator. Planck's thought was that energy was not consistent yet existed in discrete units, or quanta. He recommended that the energy of these quanta was straightforwardly corresponding to their recurrence, and this relationship became known as Planck's quantum speculation. This was a weighty takeoff from old style material science and denoted the initiation of quantum hypothesis.

Albert Einstein developed Planck's work with the photoelectric impact, recommending that light was made out of particles called photons. This speculation made sense of the noticed way of behaving of the photoelectric impact, where focusing light on a material surface caused the discharge of electrons. Photons, as per Einstein, conveyed discrete bundles of energy, and their singular still up in the air by the recurrence of the light.

As quantum hypothesis kept on creating, Niels Bohr made huge commitments by presenting quantized rakish energy in the molecule. In Bohr's nuclear model, electrons could possess explicit energy levels, or circles, around the core. Advances between these circles were quantized, and they discharged or retained energy as discrete bundles, or quanta, of electromagnetic radiation. This model effectively made sense of the unearthly lines of hydrogen and given a structure to figuring out the way of behaving of electrons in particles.

The coming of quantum mechanics as an unmistakable hypothesis is frequently credited to Werner Heisenberg and Erwin Schrödinger during the 1920s. These two physicists freely planned numerical formalisms for quantum mechanics. Heisenberg presented framework mechanics, while Schrödinger created wave mechanics. Shockingly, these apparently various methodologies were viewed as same and given a brought together system to quantum mechanics.

Heisenberg's lattice mechanics addressed quantum states as networks, while Schrödinger's wave mechanics utilized wave capabilities to portray the likelihood conveyance of particles. The wave capability, signified by the Greek letter Ψ (psi), turned into a focal idea in quantum mechanics. It permitted physicists to compute the likelihood of tracking down a molecule in a specific state or position.

One of the central standards of quantum mechanics is the wave-molecule duality, which places that particles like electrons and photons can show both wave-like and molecule like way of behaving. This duality challenges our traditional instincts, as it recommends that particles don't have unequivocal positions or speeds yet exist as likelihood circulations depicted by wave capabilities. The wave capability addresses the plentifulness of a molecule's likelihood circulation in reality.

The Schrödinger condition, created by Erwin Schrödinger, lies at the core of quantum mechanics. This differential condition portrays how the quantum condition of a framework develops over the long run.

The time-subordinate Schrödinger condition, otherwise called the Schrödinger condition, depicts the elements of quantum frameworks. It gives a method for computing how a quantum framework's wave capability changes with time and how the probabilities of various results develop.

The time-free Schrödinger condition is utilized to find the permitted energy levels and wave capabilities for a quantum framework. Tackling this condition yields a bunch of quantized energy levels for a specific quantum framework, as well as the comparing wave works that portray the likelihood conveyance of particles in those energy levels. These energy levels and wave capabilities are fundamental for grasping the way of behaving of iotas, atoms, and other quantum frameworks.

A significant idea in quantum mechanics is superposition. Superposition suggests that a quantum framework can exist in a blend of different states at the same time. This implies that a molecule can be in various places or states without a moment's delay, until it is estimated or noticed. At the point when an estimation is made, the superposition "falls" into one of the potential results, with still up in the air by the wave capability. Superposition challenges our old style instinct and recommends that particles can exist in a condition of equivocalness until they are noticed, so, all in all they expect an unmistakable state.

Another central part of quantum mechanics is the Heisenberg Vulnerability Rule, figured out by Werner Heisenberg in 1927. This standard states that it is difficult to know the specific position and energy of a molecule unhesitatingly all the while. The more precisely we know one of these properties, the less precisely we can know the other. This innate vulnerability presents a component of haphazardness and indeterminacy into the quantum world, testing the determinism of traditional material science.

Quantum mechanics additionally presents the idea of ensnarement, which is perhaps of the most fascinating and astounding peculiarity in the hypothesis. Entrapment happens when at least two particles become connected so that the condition of one molecule quickly impacts the condition of another, no matter what the distance that isolates them. This apparently non-neighborhood association has puzzled physicists and has been the subject of many examinations and discussions.

One of the key standards of quantum mechanics is quantization. Quantization implies that specific properties of a framework, for example, energy levels or rakish energy, can take on discrete, quantized values. For instance, the energy levels of electrons in a particle are quantized, meaning they can have explicit, discrete energy values. This quantization of energy levels is answerable for the discrete ghostly lines saw in nuclear spectra.

The quantization of energy levels is a consequence of the wave-like way of behaving of particles in quantum mechanics. As per the de Broglie speculation, proposed by Louis de Broglie in 1924, particles like electrons can show both molecule and wave-like properties.

The frequency related with a molecule is conversely corresponding to its energy, and that implies that particles with bigger force have more limited frequencies. This wave-molecule duality prompts the quantization of energy levels, as particles can exist in unambiguous standing wave designs inside a quantum framework.

Quantum mechanics likewise presents the idea of quantization of precise force. In the Bohr model of the hydrogen iota, for instance, the precise energy of the electron is quantized, meaning it can have specific discrete qualities. This quantization of precise force is an outcome of the quantization of energy levels in the molecule.

One of the most fascinating parts of quantum mechanics is the probabilistic idea of the hypothesis. Dissimilar to old style physical science, which gives exact determinism, quantum mechanics works in a probabilistic domain. While making estimations in quantum frameworks, we can foresee the likelihood of various results. The wave capability, which depicts the likelihood appropriation of particles, is utilized to work out these probabilities.

The Copenhagen understanding, figured out by Niels Bohr and Werner Heisenberg, is one of the most commonly known and talked about translations of quantum mechanics. As per this understanding, the demonstration of estimation or perception is integral to the breakdown of the quantum wave capability, deciding the result and driving the framework into one of the potential states. This translation underscores the job of the spectator and infers that the quantum world is innately questionable until estimated.

Notwithstanding, the Copenhagen understanding has brought up philosophical issues and discussions about the idea of the real world. It leaves the eyewitness as a key part of the interaction, prompting inquiries regarding the presence of an objective reality free of perception. This discussion has started the improvement of elective understandings, one of the most charming being the Many-Universes translation.

The Many-Universes understanding, first proposed by Hugh Everett III in quite a while, an extreme takeoff from the Copenhagen translation. As per Many-Universes, there is no breakdown of the wave capability upon estimation. All things being equal, each conceivable result of a quantum occasion happens, and every result branches into a different, non-imparting equal universe. In this translation, the universe continually branches into a limitless number of equal real factors, each addressing an alternate result of each and every quantum occasion.

In a Many-Universes situation, if you somehow managed to flip a quantum coin, the universe would part into two branches — one where the coin lands heads up and another where it lands tails up. In another model, in the event that a molecule is in a superposition of two expresses, the universe bifurcates into two particular real factors, one for every conceivable condition of the molecule. This translation recommends that all potential results are acknowledged in equal universes, making a practically boundless exhibit of existing together, non-connecting universes.

The Many-Universes translation endeavors to determine the evident mysteries and philosophical problems presented by quantum mechanics. It offers a total and deterministic portrayal of quantum occasions, where all potential results are acknowledged in discrete parts of the real world. This translation eliminates the requirement for wave capability breakdown and gives a consistent clarification to the way of behaving of particles in superposition and snare.

One of the critical qualities of the Many-Universes understanding is its capacity to give a direct and inside reliable record of quantum peculiarities. Not at all like the Copenhagen translation, which summons the baffling idea of wave capability breakdown, Many-Universes sticks to the standards of unitary development and determinism. In this structure, the Schrödinger condition generally oversees the development of quantum frameworks, without the requirement for extra hypothesizes about the job of estimation.

Many-Universes likewise offers a fantastic answer for the estimation issue, a key issue in quantum mechanics that concerns the progress from a superposition of states to a positive estimation result. In the Many-Universes understanding, this change is consistent, as all potential results are acknowledged in unmistakable parts of the real world. There is compelling reason need to summon exceptional guidelines for the job of the onlooker, as the eyewitness is just a piece of the general quantum framework.

Moreover, Many-Universes gives a rich clarification to the peculiarity of quantum ensnarement. In this translation, ensnared particles in a superposition state exist in discrete parts of the real world, it are impeccably corresponded to guarantee that their properties. The obvious non-region of snare is settled, as the particles are as of now not in a similar universe yet exist in equal branches.

In spite of its hypothetical tastefulness and allure, the Many-Universes understanding isn't without its faultfinders and difficulties. One of the essential reactions is the sheer excess of setting a boundless number of equal universes. Pundits contend that this translation presents a superfluous degree of intricacy and needs experimental proof to help the presence of these equal universes.

Also, the Many-Universes translation has confronted philosophical protests connected with the idea of individual personality and the idea of likelihood. A few pundits contend that the expansion of equal universes brings up issues about how individual character is saved as a singular settles on decisions in various parts of the real world. Others battle that the idea of likelihood becomes risky, as it is muddled the way in which probabilities are relegated across a boundless number of equal universes.

One more analysis of Many-Universes relates to its capacity to represent plainly visible items and old style conduct. While the translation is appropriate to make sense of the way of behaving of quantum particles, it turns out to be more difficult to legitimize how traditional, regular articles, like seats and vehicles, rise up out of the quantum world. Pundits contend that Many-Universes misses the mark on clear instrument for the rise of old style reality from the quantum domain.

The discussion over the Many-Universes understanding keeps on being a subject of extraordinary conversation and exploration inside the field of quantum mechanics. While it offers a rich and inside predictable system, it stays a subject of hypothesis and translation, as giving direct exploratory proof to the presence of equal universes is troublesome.

Lately, specialists have investigated the potential for exploratory trial of the Many-Universes speculation. Some have recommended that specific quantum investigations could give aberrant proof to the presence of equal universes. Be that as it may, such trials are still in the domain of hypothetical hypothesis and have not yet yielded authoritative outcomes.

One more way to deal with exploring the Many-Universes understanding is through the advancement of quantum PCs. These gadgets, which outfit the standards of quantum mechanics, can possibly play out specific estimations more effectively than traditional PCs. Some contend that the capacities of quantum PCs are demonstrative of the presence of equal universes, as these PCs exploit the quantum peculiarities on which Many-Universes is based.

As how we might interpret quantum mechanics extends, taking into account the philosophical ramifications of the Many-Universes interpretation is fundamental. This understanding difficulties our impression of the real world and the job of perception in the quantum domain. It welcomes us to mull over the idea of presence and the possibility that each quantum occasion makes a fanning tree of substitute real factors.

The Many-Universes understanding has additionally provoked conversations about the idea of awareness and the onlooker's position known to man. On the off chance that each conceivable result of a quantum occasion exists in a different universe, what's the significance here for our emotional experience of the real world? Does cognizance assume a basic part in deciding the course of our lives across these equal universes?

Besides, the Many-Universes understanding brings up issues about the idea of choice. In the event that each conceivable decision we make is acknowledged in an equal universe, do we really have the opportunity to decide, or would we say we are only following foreordained ways inside the multiverse? This philosophical scrape has extensive ramifications for how we might interpret human organization and the idea of decision.

While the Many-Universes translation offers a rich and inside reliable structure for understanding quantum mechanics, it stays a subject of progressing discussion and investigation. Its extreme takeoff from the Copenhagen translation challenges our traditional instincts and powers us to reexamine the idea of the real world, awareness, and decision.

As we peer further into the quantum domain, the secrets and mysteries of this basic hypothesis of physical science proceed to enrapture and perplex us. Quantum mechanics remains as one of the most significant and puzzling parts of science, pushing the limits of our comprehension and welcoming us to contemplate the actual embodiment of the universe. Whether we embrace the Many-Universes understanding or pick different translations, the investigation of quantum mechanics stays an excursion into the core of the quantum universe, where the unusual and the lovely coincide in an embroidery of numerical polish and philosophical interest.

3.2 Explanation of the many-worlds interpretation

The Many-Universes Translation (MWI) is an interesting and dubious understanding of quantum mechanics that proposes a revolutionary rethinking of the real world. This understanding, first planned by Hugh Everett III in quite a while, started extreme discussions and conversations in the field of physical science and reasoning. MWI challenges our conventional comprehension of quantum peculiarities and offers a remarkable point of view on the idea of the universe. In this exhaustive investigation, we will dig into the key standards, verifiable setting, and ramifications of the Many-Universes Translation.

At its center, the Many-Universes Translation proposes that quantum mechanics doesn't include the breakdown of the wave capability upon estimation, as regularly portrayed in different understandings, like the Copenhagen understanding. All things considered, MWI places that all potential results of a quantum occasion happen, each prompting the making of a different, non-conveying equal universe. At the end of the day, each time a quantum occasion occurs, the universe branches into a boundless number of equal real factors, each addressing an alternate result.

To comprehend the Many-Universes Understanding better, we should investigate its key standards and the verifiable setting where it arose.

Groundworks of the Many-Universes Translation:

MWI expands on a few critical standards of quantum mechanics, and it offers a special point of view on these standards:

Superposition: Superposition is a principal idea in quantum mechanics, which expresses that a quantum framework can exist in a blend of numerous states all the while. As such, particles can be in different places or states without a moment's delay, depicted by a superposition of potential outcomes.

Wave Capability: The wave capability is a numerical portrayal of a quantum framework that depicts the likelihood circulation of particles. In MWI, the wave capability is focal, as it addresses the plentifulness of a molecule's likelihood dissemination in reality.

Entrapment: Quantum ensnarement is a peculiarity where at least two particles become related so that the condition of one molecule momentarily impacts the condition of another, no matter what the distance that isolates them. MWI gives a translation of trap inside the setting of equal universes.

Unitary Development: In MWI, quantum frameworks advance unitarily, implying that their advancement is administered by the Schrödinger condition. The

Schrödinger condition portrays how the quantum condition of a framework changes after some time without the requirement for wave capability breakdown.

Authentic Setting:

The improvement of the Many-Universes Translation was impacted by the verifiable setting of quantum mechanics. In the mid twentieth hundred years, as quantum hypothesis was coming to fruition, a few vital trials and speculations tested the old style physical science of the time. Here are a few significant verifiable achievements that added to the rise of MWI:

Planck's Quantum Speculation (1900): Max Planck presented the possibility that energy is quantized into discrete units, or quanta. This noticeable the start of quantum hypothesis and the takeoff from old style ceaseless models.

Wave-Molecule Duality (1920s): The way of behaving of light, electrons, and different particles exhibited both wave-like and molecule like properties. This wave-molecule duality established the groundwork for the advancement of quantum mechanics.

Heisenberg's Vulnerability Rule (1927): Werner Heisenberg planned the vulnerability standard, which expresses that it is difficult to know the specific position and energy of a molecule with full confidence all the while. This brought intrinsic vulnerability and haphazardness into the quantum world.

Wave Mechanics and Network Mechanics (1920s): Erwin Schrödinger and Werner Heisenberg freely created two numerical formalisms for quantum mechanics: wave mechanics and lattice mechanics, individually. These formalisms were subsequently observed to be same and prompted the advancement of MWI.

Copenhagen Understanding (1920s): The Copenhagen translation, created by Niels Bohr and Werner Heisenberg, became one of the predominant understandings of quantum mechanics. It underscored the job of estimation and the breakdown of the wave capability upon perception.

It was in this verifiable setting of quantum hypothesis' improvement that Hugh Everett III proposed the Many-Universes Translation as an original method for figuring out the quantum world.

Key Standards of the Many-Universes Understanding:

The Many-Universes Understanding depends on a bunch of rules that recognize it from different translations of quantum mechanics. These standards assist with explaining the center thoughts of MWI:

No Breakdown of the Wave Capability: In MWI, there is no wave capability breakdown upon estimation. This is a takeoff from translations like the Copenhagen understanding, which place that estimation powers the quantum framework into a distinct state.

Stretching Universes: MWI suggests that each conceivable result of a quantum occasion happens, prompting the making of a different universe for every conceivable result. These universes are alluded to as "branches" and exist in a condition of non-correspondence.

Determinism: The Many-Universes Translation is deterministic, implying that the development of quantum frameworks is administered by the Schrödinger condition. The eventual fate of a quantum framework not entirely set in stone by its underlying circumstances and the laws of quantum mechanics.

Superposition and Ensnarement Made sense of: In MWI, superposition and trap are made sense of by the presence of numerous equal universes. At the point when a quantum framework is in superposition, it exists in numerous states, each comparing to a part of the universe. Likewise, trapped particles in various states exist in discrete branches, making sense of their relationships.

Relative State Formalism: MWI utilizes the relative state formalism to depict the connections between various parts of the universe. This formalism gives a numerical system to understanding the quantum multiverse.

Ramifications of the Many-Universes Understanding:

The Many-Universes Understanding has a few charming ramifications and outcomes, both from a logical and philosophical viewpoint:

Wave Capability Development: In MWI, the wave capability advances without interference. This intends that there is compelling reason need to summon wave capability breakdown, which is a baffling part of different translations. The Schrödinger condition generally administers the development of quantum frameworks.

Consistent Clarification of Superposition: Superposition, where particles can exist in various states all the while, is flawlessly made sense of by the presence of numerous branches in the Many-Universes Translation. Each branch relates to an unmistakable condition of the quantum framework.

Goal of the Estimation Issue: The Many-Universes Translation gives a direct answer for the estimation issue in quantum mechanics. There is compelling reason need to hypothesize the job of the spectator or present extraordinary principles for the estimation cycle. Estimations are treated as connections between the onlooker and the noticed framework.

Clarification of Quantum Snare: Quantum trap, which had been a subject of discussion and interest, is richly made sense of by MWI. Caught particles in various states are just situated in discrete branches, guaranteeing that their properties stay corresponded.

Quantum PC Capacities: The Many-Universes Translation has intriguing ramifications for quantum figuring. Quantum PCs, which tackle the standards of quantum mechanics, can play out specific computations more proficiently than traditional PCs. Some contend that the capacities of quantum PCs are characteristic of the presence of equal universes.

Difficulties and Reactions:

The Many-Universes Understanding isn't without its difficulties and reactions. A portion of the key complaints raised by physicists and savants include:

Intricacy and Luxury: Pundits contend that setting an endless number of equal universes is a luxurious and complex answer for the secrets of quantum mechanics. The presence of a limitless number of universes needs experimental proof and should be visible as a takeoff from Occam's razor, which proposes picking the most straightforward clarification when different clarifications are free.

Individual Character and Likelihood: The expansion of equal universes in MWI brings up issues about private personality. In the event that each conceivable decision we make is acknowledged in an equal universe, what's the significance here for our idea of self? Also, the idea of likelihood becomes dangerous, as it is indistinct the way in which probabilities are doled out across an endless number of equal universes.

Naturally visible Articles and Traditional Way of behaving: While the Many-Universes Translation is appropriate to make sense of the way of behaving of quantum particles, it turns out to be more difficult to legitimize how old style, ordinary items rise out of the quantum world. Pundits contend that MWI misses the mark on clear instrument for the rise of traditional reality from the quantum domain.

Testability and Experimental Proof: MWI has confronted difficulties with regards to testability and exact proof. While certain specialists have proposed exploratory tests, such tests stay in the domain of hypothetical hypothesis and have not yet yielded conclusive outcomes.

Philosophical Ramifications: The Many-Universes Translation brings up significant philosophical issues about the idea of cognizance, freedom of thought, and the idea of decision. These inquiries have extensive ramifications and remain subjects of extreme philosophical discussion.

In spite of these reactions and difficulties, the Many-Universes Understanding keeps on enamoring the creative mind of physicists and savants. It offers a convincing and inside reliable system for grasping quantum mechanics, one that pushes the limits of our old style instincts about .

3.3 The scientific basis for the existence of parallel worlds

The logical reason for the presence of equal universes, otherwise called equal universes, is a subject of progressing discussion and investigation in the field of hypothetical material science and cosmology. While the idea of equal universes might seem like sci-fi, it is grounded in a few hypothetical structures and translations of central actual standards. In this conversation, we will investigate the logical underpinnings that help equal universes, zeroing in on key speculations and understandings in physical science that have added to the idea.

1. **Many-Universes Translation of Quantum Mechanics:**
   Perhaps of the most unmistakable and dubious hypothesis that proposes the presence of equal universes is the Many-Universes Translation (MWI) of

quantum mechanics. MWI was first proposed by physicist Hugh Everett III in 1957 and offers an alternate point of view on the way of behaving of quantum frameworks.

In the Many-Universes Translation, the major reason is that quantum superposition, where a molecule can exist in various states at the same time, prompts the making of equal universes. At the point when a quantum occasion happens, all potential results are understood, and every result branches into a different, non-conveying equal universe. These universes exist in a superposition of various quantum states.

For instance, on the off chance that a quantum molecule is in a superposition of two states, one universe compares to one of those states, and the other universe relates to the next state. This translation recommends that each conceivable result of each and every quantum occasion is acknowledged in equal universes, prompting a boundless number of existing together universes.

The Many-Universes Understanding gives a numerical structure that portrays the quantum multiverse, and it depends on the Schrödinger condition, which oversees the time development of quantum frameworks. In MWI, the wave capability never falls; all things considered, it advances unitarily, guaranteeing that all potential results keep on existing in equal.

While the Many-Universes Translation is exquisite and inside steady, it stays a subject of discussion, as it presents a broad and undetectable number of equal universes. Pundits contend that it is trying to give exact proof to the presence of these equal universes, and the hypothesis' suggestions for individual character and likelihood bring up philosophical issues.

2. **Quantum Mechanics and the Superposition Guideline:**
   The logical reason for equal universes is intently attached to the crucial standards of quantum mechanics, especially the superposition rule. Quantum mechanics is the part of material science that portrays the way of behaving of issue and energy at the littlest scales, for example, the way of behaving of particles like electrons and photons.

   The superposition standard declares that quantum frameworks can exist in a blend of various states all the while. This implies that a quantum molecule can be in numerous positions or states on the double, depicted by a superposition of conceivable outcomes. The way of behaving of particles in superposition challenges traditional instincts and proposes that particles don't have distinct positions or speeds until they are estimated or noticed.

   The superposition rule is very much upheld by exploratory proof, and it assumes a focal part in quantum mechanics. It is the establishment for peculiarities like impedance, which happens when particles in superposition slow down themselves, prompting unmistakable examples in tests.

   The presence of equal universes is a characteristic result of the superposition standard. In the event that particles can exist in different states all the while, it follows that equal universes are made to oblige every conceivable state and results. Each equal universe addresses a particular arrangement of conceivable outcomes inside the quantum domain.

3. **Quantum Entrapment:**

Quantum entrapment is one more peculiarity in quantum mechanics that gives a logical premise to the idea of equal universes. Entrapment happens when at least two particles become corresponded so that the condition of one molecule immediately impacts the condition of another, no matter what the distance that isolates them. This apparently non-neighborhood association has entranced physicists and prompted conversations about the idea of the real world.

With regards to resemble universes, trapped particles in various states exist in isolated parts of the universe. The snare of particles is settled by the presence of equal universes, as every universe relates to a particular condition of the caught particles. This understanding gives a rich clarification to the connections saw in entrapment tests.

4. **Grandiose Expansion and Multiverse Speculations:**

Past quantum mechanics, the idea of equal universes is likewise connected with cosmological speculations that recommend the presence of different universes, frequently alluded to as a multiverse. One such hypothesis is vast expansion, which was acquainted with make sense of the huge scope design and homo-geneity of the universe.

As indicated by grandiose expansion hypothesis, the early universe went through a time of outstanding extension, prompting the formation of "bubble" universes inside a bigger, swelling space. These air pocket universes might have different actual constants, laws of material science, and beginning circumstances. Each air pocket universe addresses a particular locale inside the more extensive multiverse.

The idea of grandiose expansion and the multiverse is upheld by a few bits of proof, including the noticed inestimable microwave foundation radiation and the enormous scope design of the universe. While this hypothesis doesn't recommend direct correspondence between equal universes, it offers a structure for the presence of a large number of universes with different properties.

5. **String Hypothesis and the Scene:**

String hypothesis is a hypothetical system that intends to bind together the essential powers of nature and depict the way of behaving of rudimentary particles. Inside string hypothesis, there is an idea known as the "scene," which recommends the presence of countless potential vacuum states or setups.

The scene of string hypothesis suggests that our universe is only one of numerous conceivable vacuum states. Each vacuum state could relate to an alternate arrangement of actual regulations, constants, and particles. This thought prompts the idea that there could be a large number of universes inside the string hypothesis scene, each with its remarkable qualities.

While string hypothesis stays a subject of continuous exploration and discussion, the scene idea lines up with equal universes or universes with various properties.

Difficulties and Open Inquiries:

While the logical reason for equal universes is established in crucial standards of quantum mechanics and cosmological hypotheses, it is fundamental to recognize the difficulties and open inquiries related with this idea. A portion of the key difficulties include:

Exact Proof: The essential test in laying out the presence of equal universes is the absence of observational proof. Noticing or straightforwardly associating with equal universes stays past the capacities of current innovation and trial techniques. Subsequently, the idea of equal universes stays in the domain of hypothesis and speculation.

Occam's Razor: A few pundits contend that the presence of a broad number of equal universes presented by hypotheses like MWI and the multiverse opposes Occam's razor, a rule in science that proposes picking the most straightforward clarification when various clarifications are free. The idea of equal universes should be visible as excessively intricate and luxurious.

Understanding versus Reality: The presence of equal universes brings up issues about whether these universes are simply numerical builds or address actual real factors. While the Many-Universes Understanding gives a numerical structure to resemble universes, the discussion continues in regards to their ontological status.

Philosophical Ramifications: The idea of equal universes has significant philosophical ramifications, especially concerning individual character, through and through freedom, and the idea of decision. These ramifications remain subjects of extreme philosophical discussion.

String Hypothesis and Enormous Expansion: String hypothesis and grandiose expansion, while hypothetically supporting the presence of equal universes, remain subjects of progressing examination and refinement. These speculations have not been authoritatively affirmed, and their suggestions for equal universes are as yet the subject of examination.

Chapter 4

The Philosophy of Parallel Worlds

The idea of equal universes, frequently alluded to as the multiverse or many-universes understanding, is an intriguing and complex thought that has caught the minds of researchers, thinkers, and sci-fi lovers the same. It recommends that our universe is only one of many, existing in lined up with each other. This hypothesis challenges our customary comprehension of the real world and brings up significant issues about the idea of presence, cognizance, and the central rules that administer our universe.

One of the earliest notices of equal universes can be followed back to old Indian and Greek way of thinking, where the possibility of various universes was investigated as a method for making sense of the tremendous variety of human encounters and the idea of the real world. Nonetheless, it was in the twentieth century that the idea got some momentum and turned into a subject of serious logical and philosophical request.

At the core of the way of thinking of equal universes is the thought that each conceivable result and variety of occasions happens in a different universe. This implies that each choice you make, regardless of how minor or huge, prompts a fanning of the real world, with every conceivable decision unfurling in its own particular world. This thought is firmly connected with quantum mechanics, the part of material science that arrangements with the way of behaving of particles on a subatomic level.

In the realm of quantum mechanics, particles like electrons and photons can exist in numerous states on the double, a peculiarity known as superposition. Besides, the demonstration of perception or estimation implodes this superposition into a solitary state. This fascinating part of quantum mechanics led to the many-universes understanding, as it proposes that each conceivable result of a quantum occasion really happens in various parts of the multiverse.

The logician and physicist Hugh Everett III presented the many-universes understanding in 1957 as a manner to address the estimation issue in quantum mechanics. This issue spun around the vulnerability of quantum states and the job of the eyewitness in falling these states into positive results. Everett's proposition was progressive: as opposed to a solitary universe with fell quantum states, there are numerous universes, each comparing to a potential result of a quantum occasion.

One of the critical ramifications of the many-universes translation is that it dispenses with the requirement for wave capability breakdown — the cycle by which quantum probabilities become unmistakable states upon estimation.

In this view, there is no breakdown; all things considered, each conceivable result is acknowledged in a different equal universe. This translation has built up momentum among physicists, despite the fact that it stays disputable and dependent upon progressing banter.

The way of thinking of equal universes brings up significant issues about the idea of the real world and our place inside it. In the event that each conceivable decision prompts a different universe, what's the significance here with the expectation of complimentary will and determinism? Is it safe to say that we are really deciding, or would we say we are essentially exploring our direction through a generally existing large number of universes? This idea challenges our customary comprehension of causality and our capacity to impact the course of occasions.

Also, the multiverse hypothesis has profound ramifications for how we might interpret the universe. It proposes that our universe isn't interesting yet rather one among an endless number of universes, each with its own actual regulations, constants, and properties. This prompts that the circumstances forever and the development of wise creatures might shift across these universes, with some being more helpful for the presence of life as far as we might be concerned.

The idea of equal universes additionally has significant ramifications for how we might interpret cognizance. Assuming that each conceivable result is acknowledged in an equal universe, does this intend that there are endless renditions of ourselves, each encountering an alternate reality? This thought obscures the lines between private character and difficulties how we might interpret being a person.

The thought of equal universes isn't restricted to the domain of science and reasoning. It has penetrated mainstream society and sci-fi, where it has been investigated in different structures. Stories and motion pictures frequently portray characters who can go between equal universes or experience substitute adaptations of themselves. These stories offer a brief look into the psyche bowing prospects that emerge from the multiverse idea.

Notwithstanding the many-universes translation, there are different models of equal universes, each with its own extraordinary qualities and suggestions. A portion of these models are established in string hypothesis, a structure in material science that tries to accommodate general relativity and quantum mechanics. In string hypothesis, the presence of additional aspects past the natural three spatial aspects is set, and these additional aspects could bring about various universes.

One more model of equal universes is the idea of an air pocket multiverse, where our universe is only one of many air pockets drifting in an immense grandiose ocean.

Each air pocket addresses a different universe with its own arrangement of actual regulations and properties. Bubble universes offers a method for making sense of the calibrating of the constants in our universe, as each air pocket could have marginally various qualities for these constants.

The idea of the "scene" of every conceivable universe, proposed inside the structure of string hypothesis, recommends that there is a huge outfit of universes, each with its own one of a kind arrangement of actual regulations and constants. This scene of universes can be compared to an infinite library of conceivable outcomes, with our universe being only one of the many books on its racks.

One more model of equal universes is the idea of a holographic multiverse. This thought is motivated by the holographic guideline, an idea in hypothetical physical science that recommends that all the data inside a three-layered space can be encoded on a two-layered surface. In a holographic multiverse, every universe resembles a visualization, containing all the data about its whole presence on its limit.

The way of thinking of equal universes likewise meets with inquiries of presence and significance. Assuming that there are a limitless number of universes, does this deliver our singular lives and decisions irrelevant, or does it open up additional opportunities for importance and reason? This philosophical request dives into the existential ramifications of a multiverse and moves us to rethink our spot in the stupendous plan of presence.

The idea of equal universes has not been without its faultfinders and cynics. Some contend that the multiverse is a simply speculative and untestable thought, making it more a question of philosophical hypothesis than observational science. Pundits fight that without direct proof of equal universes, the idea stays in the domain of speculation and guess.

Also, a few logicians and researchers raise worries about the idea's falsifiability. That's what they contend assuming that it is basically impossible to observationally test or notice equal universes, the multiverse hypothesis might miss the mark concerning the logical basis of falsifiability, which is fundamental for a speculation to be viewed as a logical hypothesis.

Besides, the multiverse hypothesis brings up issues about the job of science and its cutoff points. Is the idea of equal universes pushing the limits of what science can really make sense of and comprehend, or is it a substantial investigation of the universe's hidden design? This discussion highlights the unique connection between science, reasoning, and the limits of human information.

Lately, there have been endeavors to test specific parts of the many-universes translation. For instance, researchers have proposed tests that could give roundabout proof to the presence of equal universes. These examinations frequently include concentrating on the way of behaving of quantum particles and testing the expectations of quantum mechanics in original ways. While the outcomes are not definitive, they add to the continuous investigation of the multiverse speculation.

The way of thinking of equal universes likewise converges with inquiries of cognizance and insight. How would we see our general surroundings, and how does our perception impact the truth we experience? The job of the onlooker in quantum mechanics, as featured by the many-universes translation, challenges how we might interpret the connection among cognizance and the outside world.

4.1 Philosophical implications of parallel worlds

The idea of equal universes, frequently connected with the multiverse hypothesis or the many-universes translation of quantum mechanics, presents a rich scene of philosophical ramifications. These ramifications address principal inquiries concerning the idea of the real world, causality, awareness, freedom of thought, personality, and the restrictions of human information. In this investigation, we dig into the philosophical parts of equal universes and the significant thoughts they cause.

At the core of the philosophical ramifications of equal universes is the idea that our universe isn't extraordinary, however one of an endless number of universes existing in equal. Every universe addresses an alternate design of the real world, an alternate arrangement of potential outcomes and results. This difficulties our customary comprehension of a particular, deterministic universe and makes the way for a large number of philosophical requests.

One of the most significant philosophical ramifications of equal universes is the test it postures to how we might interpret causality and determinism. In a conventional, single-universe view, occasions are expected to follow a direct chain of circumstances and logical results, where what's in not entirely settled by the past. In any case, in a multiverse structure, each conceivable result of an occasion happens in a different universe. This proposes that causality itself might be different in the multiverse, prompting a more perplexing and interconnected trap of circumstances and end results.

The many-universes translation of quantum mechanics, proposed by Hugh Everett III, is a great representation of this test to causality. In this understanding, quantum occasions don't prompt a solitary result however rather lead to numerous results in various universes. The job of the eyewitness in choosing one of these results further confounds how we might interpret causality and the connection among perception and reality.

This translation brings up the issue of whether choice is viable with the multiverse hypothesis. In the event that each conceivable decision prompts a stretching of the real world, do we genuinely have the ability to simply decide, or would we say we are basically exploring through a prior huge number of universes, each comparing to an alternate decision we could make? This has profound ramifications for how we might interpret human organization and the idea of direction.

The multiverse idea challenges our view of time and the idea of past, present, and future. In a multiverse, each conceivable future is acknowledged in a different universe, obscuring the qualification between what we think about the past and what's in store. This prompts inquiries regarding the progression of time and the presence of a proper course of events.

Equal universes additionally crosses with inquiries of character and individual presence. Assuming each decision we make prompts an alternate universe, does this intend that there are innumerable renditions of ourselves, each encountering an alternate reality? This idea challenges how we might interpret individual character and the idea of oneself. It brings up issues about being an individual and how we characterize our own reality.

The way of thinking of equal universes has significant ramifications for the idea of cognizance. In the event that each conceivable result of a quantum occasion is acknowledged in a different universe, does this truly intend that there are endless renditions of our cognizance, each encountering various real factors? This thought difficulties the conventional idea of a solitary, consistent continuous flow and proposes a more divided and circulated perspective on cognizance.

Besides, the multiverse hypothesis can possibly give another point of view on the idea of the real world and our place inside it. It challenges the possibility of a solitary, objective reality and makes the way for the likelihood that the truth is emotional and relative, molded by the decisions and perceptions of individual cognizance. This view reverberations components of philosophical optimism, which places that the truth is a result of the brain.

The idea of equal universes additionally meets with inquiries of morals and moral way of thinking. In the event that each conceivable decision prompts a different universe, does this intend that there are moral ramifications for our activities in every one of these universes? How does ethical quality and obligation function in a multiverse where each activity prompts a huge number of results?

Equal universes challenges how we might interpret information and logical request. Assuming there are a limitless number of universes, each with its own arrangement of actual regulations and constants, what's the significance here for the quest for logical information? Are there cutoff points to what we can be aware and grasp about the universe, given the tremendous variety of potential universes?

The multiverse hypothesis likewise brings up issues about the idea of logical truth and the job of observational proof. In a multiverse system, some have contended that the idea of equal universes may not meet the models of falsifiability — an essential rule in the way of thinking of science.

Falsifiability declares that for a theory to be viewed as logical, it should be feasible to test it and possibly refute it through exact perception or trial and error. Since the presence of equal universes is presently past the compass of direct exact proof, a few pundits contend that it may not be a logically reasonable idea.

Then again, defenders of the multiverse contend that it offers another point of view on the idea of science itself. They propose that the idea of equal universes challenges the customary limits of logical request and opens up new roads for investigating the universe. It raises doubt about the possibility that science ought to be restricted to the investigation of a solitary, deterministic universe and energizes a more far reaching perspective on the logical undertaking.

The idea of equal universes has philosophical as well as religious ramifications. It challenges conventional strict cosmologies and the possibility of a solitary, deliberate creation. The multiverse hypothesis proposes that our universe is only one of many, each with its own actual regulations and properties. This brings up issues about the uniqueness of our universe and the job of a heavenly maker in such an immense and various vast scene.

The multiverse hypothesis has ignited banters inside the domains of reasoning, science, and religious philosophy. Some contend that it is viable with strict convictions, as it considers the presence of a heavenly maker who set the boundaries for the multiverse. Others battle that it challenges strict precepts and subverts the customary thought of a solitary, deliberate universe.

The idea of equal universes has additionally tracked down its direction into mainstream society and sci-fi. Many books, films, and TV programs investigate characters going between equal universes or experiencing substitute renditions of themselves. These stories offer a brief look into the psyche bowing prospects and moral difficulties that emerge from the multiverse idea. Sci-fi has an exceptional capacity to rejuvenate dynamic philosophical thoughts and investigate their suggestions in an interesting and connecting way.

All in all, the way of thinking of equal universes, whether as the multiverse hypothesis or the many-universes understanding of quantum mechanics, presents a rich embroidery of philosophical ramifications. It challenges how we might interpret causality, time, awareness, through and through freedom, character, and the restrictions of human information. It welcomes us to reevaluate our position in the universe and our comprehension of reality itself. While the idea of equal universes stays a subject of continuous discussion and investigation, it keeps on charming the creative mind and rouse significant philosophical request.

4.2 Thought experiments and ethical considerations

Psychological tests have for quite some time been an incredible asset in way of thinking, permitting us to investigate mind boggling and dynamic thoughts by envisioning speculative situations. They assume a urgent part in moral way of thinking, where they help scholars look at and explain moral standards, situations, and moral ideas. Psychological studies in morals frequently challenge our instincts, uncover moral intricacies, and shed light on the principal inquiries of good and bad. In this investigation, we will dive into different moral psychological tests and their suggestions.

One of the most renowned moral psychological studies is the Streetcar Issue. Proposed by English savant Philippa Foot in 1967 and promoted by Judith Jarvis Thomson and Judith Jarvis Thomson in 1985, this situation presents an ethical predicament that compels us to think about the worth of human existence and the guideline of the least harmful option. In the exemplary variant of the Streetcar Issue, an out of control streetcar is made a beeline for five individuals attached to a track. You are remaining close to a switch that can redirect the streetcar onto another track, where there is just a single individual restricted. The moral inquiry is whether you ought to pull the switch to save the five at the expense of one.

The Streetcar Issue represents the strain between two moral standards: the guideline of utility, which recommends that you ought to act to limit hurt and expand generally speaking prosperity, and the rule of the holiness of life, which holds that deliberately inflicting damage is ethically off-base. It provokes our instincts and welcomes us to investigate the ethical ramifications of our activities in a day to day existence and-demise circumstance.

Varieties of the Streetcar Issue further entangle the situation. For instance, in the Footbridge rendition, you are on a footbridge sitting above the streetcar track, and you can save the five individuals by driving a huge individual over the extension, making the streetcar stop. This brings up issues about the ethical reasonability of effectively hurting forestall more prominent mischief, as well as issues of assent and the infringement of individual independence.

Another exemplary psychological study is the Ring of Gyges, depicted in Plato's Republic. In this story, a shepherd finds an otherworldly ring that awards its wearer the force of imperceptibility. The shepherd utilizes the ring to commit shameless demonstrations unafraid of outcomes. This psychological study prompts us to think about the job of results, social shows, and individual person in moral navigation.

The Ring of Gyges welcomes us to ponder whether people would act ethically in the event that they could get away from the results of their activities. It brings up issues about the idea of moral goodness, moral relativism, and the significance of accepted practices and equity in keeping up with moral way of behaving.

The idea of moral karma, presented by thinker Thomas Nagel, investigates how chance occasions can impact moral decisions. Nagel presents a situation in which two people drive carelessly, with one causing a lethal mishap, while the other tries not to hurt anybody because of sheer karma. Albeit the two drivers showed similar degree of carelessness, the ethical evaluations of their activities vary in light of the results.

Moral karma challenges our natural thoughts of decency and moral obligation. It highlights the job of karma and situation in forming our moral assessments and prompts us to consider whether we ought to pass judgment on individuals exclusively founded on their moves or likewise make into account outside factors unchangeable as far as they might be concerned.

The idea of the Shroud of Obliviousness, presented by rationalist John Rawls in his compelling work "A Hypothesis of Equity," is a psychological study intended to investigate the standards of equity. Rawls requests that we envision a situation where people are entrusted with planning an equitable society yet should do as such without information on their own societal position, riches, or position inside that society.

The Cloak of Obliviousness moves us to contemplate decency and equity from a place of unprejudiced nature, where we don't have a clue about our own conditions or honors. It prompts the improvement of the two standards of equity: the rule of equivalent fundamental freedoms and the distinction guideline, which expresses that disparities in a fair society ought to help the least advantaged.

The Shroud of Obliviousness psychological test assists us with thinking about the circulation of assets, privileges, and potential open doors in the public arena and urges us to focus on reasonableness and fairness in our moral contemplations.

One more prominent psychological test in morals is the Experience Machine, proposed by logician Robert Nozick. In this situation, you are given the choice to plug into a machine that gives a mimicked reality, undefined from this present reality, wherein you experience persistent delight and satisfaction. The catch is that you would be for all time separated from the real world and wouldn't be carrying on with a certified life.

The Experience Machine compels us to think about the worth of real encounters, independence, and the quest for joy. It challenges the decadent view that delight is a definitive wellspring of significant worth and urges us to ponder the meaning of carrying on with a significant and legitimate life, regardless of whether it incorporates enduring and challenges.

The Ticking Delayed Bomb situation is a psychological study normally utilized in conversations of morals and the morals of torment. In this situation, a fear monger has established a bomb in a populated region, and there's simply no time left. The best way to forestall the blast and save blameless lives is to torment the caught fear monger to get data about the bomb's area.

The Ticking Delayed Bomb situation brings up significant moral issues about the utilization of torment in outrageous circumstances. It compels us to gauge the worth of basic freedoms and moral standards against the basic to forestall hurt and safeguard blameless lives. This psychological test is much of the time discussed, with some contending that it shows the ethical intricacy of certifiable moral problems, while others battle that it works on an intricate issue.

The idea of the Boat of Theseus is a psychological study that investigates the idea of character and individual personality. The situation includes a boat, the Boat of Theseus, which progressively has every one of its parts supplanted over the long haul. Assuming that all aspects of the boat is supplanted, is it as yet unchanged boat?

The Boat of Theseus brings up issues about the tirelessness of character and the idea of individual personality. It welcomes us to consider whether character is attached to the progression of actual parts or on the other hand in the event that it is a more unique and persevering through idea. This psychological study is pertinent to conversations about private character, oneself, and the philosophical issue of personality after some time.

The psychological study known as the Principle of Twofold Impact is frequently used to investigate the profound quality of activities that have both great and awful results. In this situation, an activity is performed fully intent on accomplishing a decent result yet in addition brings about an accidental terrible result.

The Regulation of Twofold Impact assists us with assessing the passability of activities that include moral difficulties, where a good natured act prompts accidental mischief. It moves us to think about the job of expectation, premonition, and the proportionality of good and terrible results in moral direction.

The idea of the Detainee's Problem, frequently utilized in game hypothesis and morals, presents a situation where two people should choose whether to participate or double-cross one another. The quandary features the pressure between individual personal circumstance and the aggregate interest of the two players.

The Detainee's Predicament brings up issues about trust, participation, and the soundness of moral navigation. It shows the difficulties of accommodating individual increase with the benefit of everyone and fills in as a model for investigating the elements of participation and rivalry in different social and moral settings.

The moral psychological study known as the Awfulness of the House investigates the outcomes of people seeking after their personal circumstance without respect for a long term benefit. In a situation where various people share a typical asset, like a field, oneself intrigued activities of every individual lead to the consumption and debasement of the asset, eventually hurting everybody.

4.3 The role of parallel worlds in discussions of determinism and free will

The idea of equal universes, frequently connected with the multiverse hypothesis or the many-universes understanding of quantum mechanics, assumes a critical part in conversations of determinism and through and through freedom. These essential philosophical ideas have been at the core of discussions for quite a long time, and the presence of equal universes acquaints new layers of intricacy with these conversations. In this investigation, we will dig into the complicated connection between equal universes, determinism, and through and through freedom.

Determinism, in its most straightforward structure, is the possibility that all occasions, including human activities and decisions, are foreordained and can be made sense of by the circumstances and occasions that go before them. It recommends that there is a whole chain of causality that oversees the universe, ruling out evident arbitrariness or indeterminacy. Determinism can take different structures, for example,

Causal Determinism: This type of determinism declares that each not entirely settled by going before occasions in a causal chain. In this view, what's to come is very much unsurprising assuming one knows the underlying circumstances and the regulations that oversee these causal connections.

Philosophical Determinism: A few strict tenets suggest that a heavenly being has foreordained all occasions, including human decisions, in light of a heavenly arrangement. This viewpoint brings up issues about human unrestrained choice despite divine destiny.

Coherent Determinism: This view recommends that the rule of bivalence, which affirms that each assertion is either obvious or misleading, decides the result of every future occasion and activities. In this sense, what's in store is as of still up in the air.

The idea of equal universes essentially affects determinism since it challenges the possibility of a solitary, straight course of events. If the multiverse hypothesis is valid, with every quantum occasion prompting a spreading of reality into numerous universes, then the conventional idea of a particular, deterministic timetable is raised doubt about. The presence of equal universes suggests that each conceivable result of a quantum occasion is acknowledged in discrete universes, prompting a more complicated and interconnected snare of causality.

With regards to quantum mechanics, the many-universes understanding recommends that particles, for example, electrons and photons, exist in superpositions of numerous states until they are noticed. At the point when noticed, these superpositions breakdown into a solitary state.

In the many-universes translation, as opposed to a solitary breakdown, each conceivable result of a quantum occasion happens in various parts of the multiverse. This brings up issues about the idea of causality and the job of perception in deciding results.

Pundits of determinism contend that the presence of equal universes challenges the deterministic perspective. In a multiverse, the result of a quantum occasion isn't particular however various, with every result acknowledged in a different universe. This proposes that what's in store isn't foreordained in a solitary, unalterable way yet is rather portrayed by a huge number of potential fates. This has driven some to contend that the multiverse hypothesis presents a component of indeterminacy at the quantum level.

In any case, defenders of determinism fight that the idea of equal universes doesn't be guaranteed to subvert the general rule of causality. They contend that the stretching of reality in a multiverse is as yet a consequence of deterministic cycles, like quantum mechanics. While it presents intricacy and a large number of results, these results are not entirely set in stone by the laws of physical science and the underlying states of the universe. All in all, determinism works inside each part of the multiverse, prompting different deterministic results in various universes.

Determinism likewise brings up issues about the idea of unrestrained choice. Freedom of thought is the idea that people have the ability to simply decide and choices that still up in the air by outside powers, like destiny or fate. It suggests that people have the ability to act as indicated by their own cravings and goals, no matter what the deterministic cycles that administer the universe.

The connection among determinism and freedom of thought has been a subject of longstanding philosophical discussion. A few contend that determinism and freedom of thought are incongruent, as the possibility of a foreordained universe appears to rule out veritable decision or independence. Assuming each occasion and activity is foreordained by the past, it might appear to be that people are simple manikins in an enormous play, following a content composed by the underlying states of the universe.

The presentation of equal universes into this discussion adds a layer of intricacy. In a multiverse, the subject of freedom of thought becomes caught with the topic of which "you" is pursuing the decision. In the event that each conceivable decision prompts a spreading of reality into isolated universes, each comparing to an alternate decision, it challenges our ordinary comprehension of individual organization. It brings up the issue of whether you are really pursuing a decision, or on the other hand if every variant of "you" is just following a foreordained way in its separate universe.

Pundits of freedom of thought contend that the multiverse hypothesis, by inferring a huge number of foreordained results for every decision, sabotages the idea of veritable choice. They fight that through and through freedom, as generally comprehended, requires the capacity to pursue decisions that not entirely set in stone by earlier circumstances or outside factors. In a multiverse, the presence of equal universes recommends that each decision you make is foreordained in some universe, ruling out obvious independence.

Advocates of freedom of thought, then again, keep up with that the idea of equal universes doesn't be guaranteed to invalidate the chance of choice. They contend that through and through freedom isn't dependent upon the presence of equal universes yet rather on the limit of people to go with decisions in view of their own longings, aims, and thinking. In this view, the presence of equal universes is superfluous to the topic of through and through freedom, as freedom of thought is an idea that relates to the person's emotional experience of decision.

The discussion over the similarity of determinism and freedom of thought is continuous and stays a mind boggling and petulant issue in way of thinking. While equal universes acquaint new aspects with this discussion, they don't give a conclusive goal to the essential inquiries encompassing human organization and the idea of decision.

The idea of equal universes additionally meets with the philosophical issue of individual character. If each decision prompts a spreading of the real world, does this truly intend that there are innumerable renditions of "you," each encountering an alternate reality? This difficulties our customary comprehension of individual way of life as a constant and particular self.

The idea of individual character has been a focal topic in philosophical conversations for a really long time, with questions, for example, "What makes you a similar individual you were previously?" and "What comprises the center of your personality?" being subjects of discussion. The presence of equal universes acquaints new aspects with these inquiries, as it recommends that individual personality may not be basically as steady and solitary as recently suspected.

The way of thinking of individual personality can be separated into different speculations, including:

Mental Progression Hypothesis: This hypothesis sets that individual character depends on the coherence of mental qualities, like recollections, awareness, and character attributes. In a multiverse, the test is to figure out which rendition of a person in an alternate universe can be viewed as the "same" individual in light of mental congruity.

Natural Hypothesis: A few thinkers contend that individual character is grounded in the organic congruity of the person. In a multiverse, the inquiry emerges regarding how different organic forms of a person in equal universes connect with their own character.

Story Character Hypothesis: As per this hypothesis, individual personality is developed through the account of one's life. Each fanning of reality in a multiverse might actually create a particular life story, bringing up issues about which account characterizes a singular's personality.

The presence of equal universes challenges these speculations of individual character, as it recommends that there might be numerous variants of an individual, each with its own mental, organic, and story qualities. This brings up the issue of whether individual personality is essentially as fixed and particular as customarily expected, or on the other hand on the off chance that it is more flexible and circulated across equal universes.

The philosophical ramifications of equal universes additionally stretch out to inquiries of moral obligation and responsibility. Assuming there are endless renditions of people pursuing various decisions in equal universes, does this imply that every adaptation bears moral obligation regarding their activities? How would we credit moral culpability in a multiverse where each conceivable decision is understood?

The test of moral obligation in a multiverse is especially obvious in psychological studies like the Streetcar Issue. In this situation, the choice to pull a switch and redirect a streetcar to save five individuals to the detriment of one includes moral ramifications. In the event that each decision prompts a spreading of the truth, are there endless variants of people who settled on various decisions in comparative circumstances? Should this large number of adaptations be considered ethically answerable for their decisions?

Additionally, the idea of equal universes brings up issues about the idea of morals and the objectivity of moral standards. Assuming there are limitless universes, each with its own arrangement of moral qualities and standards, does this imply that morals is emotional and relative? How would we accommodate the variety of moral frameworks across equal universes with the possibility of genuine moral bits of insight?

Chapter 5

Science Fiction and Parallel Realities

Sci-fi has forever been a class that pushes the limits of human creative mind. It permits us to investigate universes that are incomprehensibly unique in relation to our own, or to imagine what our future could resemble. Quite possibly of the most captivating and mind-bowing idea in sci-fi is equal real factors or substitute aspects. These are universes that exist close by our own, however with various guidelines, various chronicles, and various results. The idea of equal real factors has caught the creative mind of creators, producers, and researchers the same, and it has been a common subject in sci-fi for quite a long time.

At the core of the idea of equal truths is the possibility that our universe isn't the one to focus on. Truth be told, there could be a limitless number of universes, each with its own arrangement of actual regulations, constants, and real factors. This hypothesis, known as the "multiverse" speculation, has gotten forward momentum lately, in spite of the fact that it stays a subject of discussion among physicists and cosmologists. In the multiverse, each possible reality exists some place, from an existence where dinosaurs actually meander the Earth to one where people have accomplished idealistic social orders.

One of the earliest works of sci-fi to investigate equal truths is H.G. Wells' "The Time Machine," distributed in 1895. In this novel, the hero designs a machine that permits him to go through time and witness various periods of Earth's set of experiences. While the book doesn't expressly dig into equal real factors, it brings up the issue of what could occur in the event that one could control time and steer history. Wells' original sowed the seed for the investigation of substitute real factors in sci-fi.

As the class advanced, creators started to straightforwardly handle the idea of equal real factors more. Philip K. Dick, a productive sci-fi essayist, was known for his investigation of substitute aspects in works like "The Man in the High Palace" and "Ubik." In "The Man in the High Palace," Dick imagines a world wherein the Pivot powers won The Second Great War, bringing about something else entirely scene. The novel investigates how people in this substitute reality see their reality and adapt to the real factors of an altogether different history.

Dick's work was instrumental in advocating that the truth is emotional and can shift starting with one individual then onto the next, even inside a similar universe. This idea of emotional reality and various layers of presence turned into a sign of his composition and impacted numerous resulting sci-fi creators.

Another exemplary work that digs into equal truths is Lewis Carroll's "Alice's Experiences in Wonderland." While not customary sci-fi, this fantastical story takes Alice on an excursion through a peculiar and strange world. As Alice experiences talking creatures, evolving sizes, and a huge number of silly characters, obviously Wonderland works under a bunch of rules totally not the same as our own world. Carroll's story should be visible as an early investigation of equal real factors, where the normal laws of material science and rationale are suspended.

During the twentieth 100 years, creators like Isaac Asimov and Arthur C. Clarke started to investigate the idea of equal real factors from a more logical point of view. Asimov's "The Finish of Endlessness" presented the idea of "Forever," an association that could control time and make substitute real factors by changing key crossroads ever. This novel digs into the moral and philosophical ramifications of such power, bringing up issues about the outcomes of altering the past.

Arthur C. Clarke's "Youth's End" investigates progressed outsider creatures regulating human development and directing mankind towards another phase of presence. This novel addresses topics of greatness and the change of human culture, offering a brief look into an equal reality where the predetermination of humanity follows an alternate way.

During the 1960s and 1970s, the investigation of equal real factors in sci-fi took on new aspects with the ascent of the nonconformity and the hallucinogenic development. Creators like Robert Anton Wilson and Philip Jose Rancher pushed the limits of the real world and awareness in their works. Wilson's "The Illuminatus! Set of three" is a great representation of writing that obscures the lines between paranoid notions, substitute real factors, and the view of truth.

The 1980s and 1990s achieved a resurgence of interest in equal real factors in sci-fi. The TV series "Sliders" follows a gathering of voyagers who utilize a gadget to jump between equal Earths, each with its own interesting qualities. The show investigates how little changes in history can prompt tremendously various results, outlining the butterfly impact in real life.

In the mean time, the "Star Trip" establishment presented the idea of the "reflect universe," where the recognizable characters of the Starship Venture exist in a dull and dictator substitute reality. This equal universe turned into a common topic in different Star Journey series and featured the duality of human instinct.

The 21st century has seen a proceeded with interest with equal real factors in sci-fi. The movie "Origin" coordinated by Christopher Nolan investigates shared dreaming and the control of reality inside dreams. The story obscures the line among dream and reality, making a story that works on various degrees of presence.

A later model is the TV series "The Man in the High Palace," in view of Philip K. Dick's novel, which imagines an other reality where the Pivot powers won The Second Great War and the US is split between the Nazis and the Japanese.

The series dives into the political and social results of such a situation and the battle for opposition in reality as we know it where history took an alternate course.

The idea of equal real factors has additionally found its direction into computer games, with titles like "Bioshock Limitless" and "Quantum Break" offering players the chance to investigate substitute aspects and pursue decisions that influence the game's result. These intelligent encounters carry equal real factors to another level, permitting players to take part in molding the story effectively.

Equal truths are not restricted to the domain of diversion and fiction; they certainly stand out of researchers and rationalists. The idea of the multiverse, as proposed in different hypothetical structures, recommends that our universe is only one of numerous inside a huge grandiose troupe. In the multiverse speculation, every universe might have different actual regulations, constants, and starting circumstances, prompting a huge number of assorted real factors.

One variant of the multiverse hypothesis is the "many-universes understanding" of quantum mechanics, which recommends that each quantum occasion brings about the expanding of new universes, each addressing an alternate result of that occasion. This translation suggests that there are endless equal real factors continually separating from our own, and each conceivable result of any quantum cooperation happens in one of these real factors.

While the many-universes understanding remaining parts a subject of discussion and isn't generally acknowledged among physicists, an entrancing and mind-twisting thought lines up with the idea of equal real factors in sci-fi. The equal real factors in the many-universes understanding are unique ideas as well as potential actual real factors that exist close by our own.

As science and innovation advance, the investigation of equal real factors keeps on developing. The field of augmented reality permits people to submerge themselves in computerized universes that can copy or veer off from our own world. Increased reality innovation overlays computerized data on the actual world, making a type of equal reality where advanced and actual components coincide.

In the domain of quantum figuring, scientists are investigating the possibility to saddle the force of quantum mechanics to perform computations that would be unthinkable with traditional PCs. Quantum PCs could hypothetically recreate and investigate equal real factors, empowering new experiences into quantum peculiarities and complex frameworks.

In the field of man-made consciousness, there is continuous examination into establishing virtual specialists and reenacted conditions that can imitate human way of behaving and thought. These virtual creatures could exist in equal real factors inside the computerized domain, collaborating with people and possibly forming how we might interpret awareness and knowledge.

The investigation of equal truths isn't restricted to the physical and computerized domains; it likewise reaches out to the domain of reasoning and mysticism. Logicians have long contemplated inquiries regarding the idea of the real world and the presence of numerous aspects or planes of presence.

The idea of equal real factors brings up significant philosophical issues about the idea of truth, discernment, and oneself. Assuming that there are endless equal real factors, each with its own rendition of occasions and people, how might we at any point figure out what is equitably obvious? Does the presence of equal real factors sabotage the idea of a solitary, objective reality?

The philosophical investigation of equal real factors likewise dives into the possibility of individual character. In the event that each decision we make brings about a fanning of real factors, there are endless variants of ourselves in various equal universes. This difficulties our regular comprehension of selfhood and brings up issues about the idea of character and awareness.

In the domain of religion and otherworldliness, the idea of equal real factors has matches with convictions in numerous aspects, higher planes of presence, and substitute domains possessed by divinities, spirits, or other powerful creatures. Numerous strict.

5.1 The role of science fiction in popularizing the concept

The job of sci-fi in advocating the idea of equal truths is both significant and diverse. Since its origin, sci-fi has filled in as a stage for investigating and spreading perplexing and theoretical thoughts. Equal real factors, substitute aspects, and multiverses are ideas that have caught the creative mind of the two makers and crowds. Sci-fi plays had an essential impact in acquainting these thoughts with a more extensive crowd, molding our social comprehension of them, and in any event, affecting logical idea and examination.

Sci-fi, as a kind, has frequently been at the very front of presenting and promoting new logical and philosophical ideas. The class gives an innovative space where creators, producers, and different makers can push the limits of human creative mind and investigate what is conceivable past the requirements of current information. Equal real factors, specifically, offer a material for boundless investigation.

One of the manners in which sci-fi has promoted the idea of equal truths is by giving distinctive and connecting with stories that make the thought open and engaging to a wide crowd. At the point when introduced as a story, complex logical or philosophical thoughts become more receptive and enrapturing. Perusers and watchers can associate with the characters, settings, and situations introduced in these accounts, which assists them with embracing the complexities of the idea.

H.G. Wells' "The Time Machine," distributed in 1895, is one of the earliest instances of a sci-fi work that digs into the idea of equal real factors. In spite of the fact that it fundamentally centers around time travel, it brings up issues about the chance of modifying the direction of history and, likewise, making substitute real factors. Wells' story presents the possibility of a machine that can move its administrator to various moments, successfully permitting them to observe and communicate with elective chronicles. While the novel doesn't expressly investigate equal aspects, it plants the seeds of hypothesis about what could occur in the event that time could be controlled to make various real factors.

Equal real factors likewise show up in crafted by Philip K. Dick, a productive and compelling sci-fi creator. His book "The Man in the High Palace" investigates a world where the Hub powers won The Second Great War and hence split the US between the Nazis and the Japanese. The clever offers a clear depiction of an equal reality, where verifiable situation unfurled in an unexpected way, bringing about a profoundly changed international scene. The story furnishes perusers with a brief look into how individuals in this substitute world see their current circumstance, wrestle with moral difficulties, and adjust to the real factors of an unmistakable history.

Moreover, Philip K. Dick's book "Ubik" presents a reality-twisting story that challenges the limits of insight and presence. In this story, the characters experience odd and moving real factors, obscuring the lines between what is genuine and what isn't. "Ubik" epitomizes how sci-fi can connect with perusers in provocative investigations of abstract reality and the pliability of discernment.

Lewis Carroll's "Alice's Experiences in Wonderland," while not rigorously a sci-fi work, can be viewed as an early investigation of equal real factors. In this fantastical story, Alice sets out on an excursion through a strange and counter-intuitive reality where the common laws of physical science and rationale don't make a difference. The story acquaints perusers with a domain where the limits of the truth are liquid, and the surprising is the standard. "Alice's Experiences in Wonderland" challenges how we might interpret reality and offers a creative forerunner to later, more expressly sci-fi investigations of equal aspects.

As sci-fi developed during the twentieth hundred years, creators started to handle the idea of equal real factors all the more straightforwardly, frequently integrating components of quantum physical science and hypothetical science. Isaac Asimov's "The Finish of Endlessness" acquainted perusers with the possibility of an association equipped for controlling chance to make substitute real factors by changing crucial points in time ever. Asimov's original brings up moral and philosophical issues about the ramifications of messing with the past and modifying the direction of occasions. By meshing this idea into a convincing story, Asimov promoted the thought of equal real factors as a subject for investigation.

Arthur C. Clarke's "Youth's End" adopts an alternate strategy to resemble real factors by investigating the mediation of cutting edge outsider creatures in human development. In this novel, these extraterrestrial elements guide mankind towards another phase of presence, testing the traditional direction of mankind's set of experiences. "Youth's End" expresses a viewpoint inciting vision of how humankind's predetermination could separate in an other reality, pushing perusers to consider the potential outcomes of an alternate future.

All through the 1960s and 1970s, sci-fi's investigation of equal real factors extended as the class developed and retained impacts from the nonconformity and the hallucinogenic development. Creators like Robert Anton Wilson and Philip Jose Rancher presented components of psyche extending encounters, paranoid notions, and changed conditions of awareness into their works. These accounts frequently obscured the lines between the real world, dream, and equal aspects, mirroring the period's interest with unpredictable and otherworldly ideas.

Robert Anton Wilson's "The Illuminatus! Set of three" encapsulates the non-conformity's hug of substitute real factors and conspiratorial reasoning. The set of three mixes components of paranoid ideas, substitute aspects, and the quest for buried insights. The story provokes perusers to scrutinize the idea of the real world, the unwavering quality of data, and the limits of human discernment.

The 1980s and 1990s saw a resurgence of interest in equal real factors, both in writing and on screen. The TV series "Sliders" follows a gathering of explorers who utilize a gadget to bounce between equal Earths, each with its own extraordinary qualities and chronicles. The show investigates how little changes in history can prompt tremendously various results, outlining the butterfly impact in real life. "Sliders" enamored crowds with its investigation of assorted real factors and the ethical issues that emerge from adjusting authentic occasions.

In the "Star Trip" establishment, the idea of the "reflect universe" was presented, offering an equal reality where natural characters from the Starship Venture existed in a dull and tyrant substitute world. This repetitive subject in different "Star Trip" series tested the duality of human instinct, as characters experienced their partners in the mirror universe and wrestled with the possibility that their decisions had prompted unique predeterminations.

The 21st century got a new rush of interest equal real factors, with sci-fi proceeding to push the limits of creative mind and investigate new features of this idea. Christopher Nolan's film "Origin" dives into the control of reality inside dreams. The account obscures the line among dream and reality, making a story that works on various layers of presence. "Commencement" welcomes watchers to explore a labyrinth of moving real factors and question the limits of cognizance.

Another critical work that investigates equal truths is the TV series "The Man in the High Palace," in view of Philip K. Dick's book. The series imagines an other reality where the Pivot powers won The Second Great War, prompting a partitioned US.

Watchers are drenched in a world with radically unique political and social scenes, and they witness the battles of those opposing the laid out request. "The Man in the

High Palace" offers a provocative depiction of how an alternate verifiable result can shape the course of humankind.

Equal real factors have likewise found a spot in the realm of computer games. Titles, for example, "Bioshock Boundless" and "Quantum Break" permit players to investigate substitute aspects and pursue decisions that impact the game's result. These intuitive encounters enable players to effectively take part in molding the account, adding a connecting with and vivid aspect to the idea of equal real factors.

While sci-fi has without a doubt assumed a urgent part in promoting the idea of equal real factors, it has not been restricted to the domain of fiction and diversion. The possibility of the multiverse, which incorporates equal real factors as a subset, has built up forward movement in logical conversations and hypothetical physical science. The multiverse speculation places that our universe is only one of many, each with its remarkable arrangement of actual regulations, constants, and real factors.

One conspicuous adaptation of the multiverse hypothesis is the "many-universes understanding" of quantum mechanics. This translation recommends that each quantum occasion brings about the production of new universes, each addressing an alternate result of that occasion. Basically, the many-universes translation suggests that a limitless number of equal real factors exist, continually fanning out from our own with each quantum communication.

While the many-universes translation stays a subject of discussion among physicists and has not accomplished general acknowledgment, it addresses an entrancing and mind-twisting thought that adjusts intimately with the idea of equal real factors investigated in sci-fi. The equal real factors in the many-universes translation are not only conceptual ideas but rather potential actual real factors that exist close by our own.

The idea of equal real factors has likewise advanced into the fields of quantum figuring and man-made consciousness. Quantum registering, specifically, holds the commitment of mimicking and investigating equal real factors. By saddling the standards of quantum mechanics, quantum PCs can perform estimations that would be infeasible for traditional PCs. These high level machines could be utilized to recreate quantum peculiarities and complex frameworks, possibly revealing insight into the idea of equal aspects and the secrets of the quantum world.

In the field of computerized reasoning, scientists are chipping away at establishing virtual specialists and reproduced conditions that can impersonate human way of behaving and thought.

These virtual creatures could exist in equal real factors inside the computerized domain, connecting with people and adding to how we might interpret cognizance and knowledge. The advancement of these virtual substances obscures the line among the real world and reproduction, offering new chances to investigate the idea of equal real factors.

The investigation of equal truths isn't restricted to the physical and advanced domains; it additionally stretches out into the domains of reasoning and mysticism.

Thinkers have long examined inquiries concerning the idea of the real world, presence, and the presence of various aspects or planes of being. The idea of equal real factors raises significant philosophical requests that challenge customary thoughts of truth, discernment, and character.

One of the crucial philosophical inquiries raised by the idea of equal truths is the idea of truth. Assuming a boundless number of equal real factors exist, each with its special adaptation of occasions and people, how might we at any point discover what is impartially evident? The presence of equal real factors can challenge the possibility of a solitary, objective reality and brief a reevaluation of how we characterize truth and reality itself.

The idea of equal real factors additionally converges with the way of thinking of discernment and epistemology. On the off chance that various real factors can coincide close by our own, each with its unmistakable arrangement of realities and encounters, it brings up issues about the idea of discernment and the unwavering quality of our faculties. How might we trust our insights on the off chance that they can fluctuate across various equal real factors? This philosophical investigation welcomes us to ponder the constraints of human information and the intricacies of the world as we see it.

Moreover, equal real factors challenge customary thoughts of individual personality. In the event that each decision we make brings about an expanding of real factors, there are endless forms of ourselves in various equal universes, each going with various choices and confronting different conditions. This idea challenges how we might interpret selfhood and prompts us to scrutinize the idea of personality and awareness. It raises the fascinating chance that individual personality is definitely not a perpetual and solitary idea yet a diverse and developing one that exists in lined up across different real factors.

Equal real factors additionally converge with strict and otherworldly convictions. Numerous strict and otherworldly practices set the presence of real factors past the actual world, which are frequently viewed as crossing with or impacting our own existence. These convictions include the idea of higher planes of presence, substitute domains possessed by divinities, spirits, or other powerful creatures.

In a few strict and profound practices, people try to get to or rise above these equal real factors through contemplation, modified conditions of cognizance, or customs. These practices are expected to interface with divine creatures, look for direction, or gain understanding into the secrets of presence.

The confidence in equal aspects, substitute real factors, and higher planes of being has significant ramifications for the comprehension of otherworldliness and the human association with the heavenly.

The idea of equal real factors has likewise tracked down its direction into mainstream society and folklore. Metropolitan legends and old stories frequently highlight stories of secretive gateways to different aspects or substitute universes. These accounts reverberate with the human interest for the obscure and the chance of extraordinary encounters. These legends catch the pith of equal real factors as spots of experience, secret, and change.

All in all, the job of sci-fi in promoting the idea of equal truths is obviously huge. Sci-fi has filled in as an inventive and creative stage for presenting, investigating, and dispersing perplexing and speculative thoughts regarding equal aspects, substitute real factors, and the multiverse. Through striking stories, sci-fi has made these theoretical and logical ideas open to a wide crowd, empowering perusers and watchers to draw in with the thoughts and question how they might interpret reality.

From the early works of H.G. Wells to the psyche bowing stories of Philip K. Dick and contemporary sci-fi, equal real factors have been a repetitive subject that challenges our regular thoughts of the real world, insight, and presence. While sci-fi frequently works in the domain of hypothesis and creative mind, it has likewise affected logical idea and exploration, especially in the fields of quantum physical science, cosmology, and quantum processing.

The idea of equal real factors welcomes us to investigate the limitless potential outcomes that might exist just outside our ability to understand. It urges us to dream, to ponder, and to think about the endless capability of the human creative mind. As science and innovation keep on propelling, the investigation of equal real factors stays a dynamic and developing subject that will without a doubt shape how we might interpret the universe and our place inside it. Sci-fi will keep on being an indispensable conductor for these thoughts, enhancing our social scene and moving new ages to consider the secrets of equal real factors.

5.2 Iconic sci-fi stories featuring parallel worlds

Notorious sci-fi stories including equal universes have for some time been a staple of the class. These stories take perusers and watchers on mind-bowing excursions through substitute aspects, offering looks at universes where the standards of the truth are unique, authentic occasions have gone off in strange directions, and characters face novel difficulties. These accounts have made a permanent imprint on sci-fi, dazzling crowds with their investigation of equal real factors. In this investigation of notorious science fiction stories, we'll dig into a few remarkable works that have promoted and characterize the idea of equal universes.

One of the earliest and most getting through instances of equal world investigation in sci-fi is Lewis Carroll's "Alice's Undertakings in Wonderland," distributed in 1865. While not a customary sci-fi work, Carroll's story acquaints perusers with a capricious and counter-intuitive world that works under its own exceptional arrangement of rules. At the point when Alice tumbles down a deep, dark hole, she enters a fantastical domain where creatures talk, sizes change freely, and rationale takes a secondary lounge to ludicrousness. Wonderland is an equal world that challenges the limits of the real world and welcomes perusers to suspend their skepticism. Carroll's work laid the foundation for some other time, all the more unequivocally sci-fi investigations of equal aspects.

H.G. Wells' "The Time Machine," distributed in 1895, is one more early illustration of a sci-fi work that clues at the idea of equal real factors. While the novel essentially investigates time travel, it brings up issues about the chance of modifying the direction of history and, likewise, making substitute real factors. In the story, the hero concocts a machine that permits him to go through time and witness various periods of Earth's set of experiences. While the book doesn't expressly dive into equal aspects, it sows the seed for the investigation of substitute real factors by presenting controlling chance to make various results.

As the sci-fi type kept on developing, creators started to straightforwardly handle the idea of equal real factors more. Philip K. Dick, a productive sci-fi essayist known for his investigation of substitute aspects, acquainted perusers with the possibility of emotional reality and different layers of presence. His book "Ubik," distributed in 1969, is a great representation of his work in such manner. In "Ubik," the characters experience unusual and moving real factors, obscuring the lines between what is genuine and what isn't. The story challenges the limits of discernment and the pliability of the real world, making it a quintessential investigation of equal universes.

Philip K. Dick's "The Man in the High Palace," distributed in 1962, is another notorious work that imagines a reality where the Pivot powers won The Second Great War, bringing about an unfathomably different international scene. The novel investigates how people in this substitute reality see their reality and adapt to the real factors of a totally different history. "The Man in the High Palace" expresses perusers a viewpoint inciting look into an equal reality where verifiable occasions took an other course, passing on the characters to wrestle with the outcomes.

Isaac Asimov, a light in the realm of sci-fi, likewise dug into the idea of equal real factors with his book "The Finish of Forever," distributed in 1955. In this story, Asimov acquaints perusers with the idea of "Forever," an association with the ability to control time and make substitute real factors by changing essential crossroads ever. The novel digs into the moral and philosophical ramifications of messing with the past and changing the direction of occasions, filling in as a provocative investigation of equal aspects.

Arthur C. Clarke's "Youth's End," distributed in 1953, investigates progressed outsider creatures regulating human development and directing mankind toward another phase of presence. The clever difficulties the regular direction of mankind's set of experiences, offering perusers a brief look into how the fate of humanity could follow an alternate way in a substitute reality. "Youth's End" is a fundamental work that welcomes perusers to consider the conceivable outcomes of an alternate future and the job of outside powers in molding equal universes.

The 1980s and 1990s saw a resurgence of interest in equal real factors in sci-fi. The TV series "Sliders," which broadcasted from 1995 to 2000, follows a gathering of voyagers who utilize a gadget to jump between equal Earths, each with its own extraordinary qualities and narratives. The show investigates how little changes in history can prompt immeasurably various results, representing the butterfly impact in real life. "Sliders" spellbound crowds with its investigation of assorted real factors and the ethical problems that emerge from adjusting verifiable occasions.

The "Star Trip" establishment, with its various series and movies, presented the idea of the "reflect universe." This equal the truth is a repetitive topic all through different "Star Journey" emphasess, where natural characters from the Starship Endeavor exist in a dim and dictator substitute world. The presence of the mirror universe challenges the duality of human instinct, as characters experience their partners and wrestle with the possibility that their decisions have prompted unique fates. "Star Journey" exhibits the persevering through allure of equal real factors as a story gadget inside sci-fi.

The 21st century got a new rush of interest equal real factors in sci-fi, with works that kept on testing the limits of creative mind and investigate new features of the idea. Christopher Nolan's film "Origin," delivered in 2010, dives into the control of reality inside dreams. The account obscures the line among dream and reality, making a story that works on various layers of presence. "Commencement" welcomes watchers to explore a labyrinth of moving real factors and question the limits of cognizance.

A later illustration of sci-fi investigating equal truths is the TV series "The Man in the High Palace," which appeared in 2015. In view of Philip K. Dick's novel, the series imagines an other reality where the Pivot powers won The Second Great War, prompting a separated US. Watchers are submerged in a world with definitely unique political and social scenes, and they witness the battles of those opposing the laid out request. "The Man in the High Palace" offers a provocative depiction of how an alternate verifiable result can shape the course of humankind.

Equal real factors have likewise advanced into the domain of computer games. Titles, for example, "Bioshock Limitless," delivered in 2013, and "Quantum Break," delivered in 2016, permit players to investigate substitute aspects and go with decisions that impact the game's result. These intelligent encounters enable players to effectively take part in molding the story, adding a drawing in and vivid aspect to the idea of equal real factors.

While sci-fi has without a doubt assumed a urgent part in promoting the idea of equal real factors, it has not been bound to the domain of fiction and diversion. The possibility of the multiverse, which envelops equal real factors as a subset, has gotten some momentum in logical conversations and hypothetical material science. The multiverse speculation recommends that our universe is only one of numerous inside a tremendous inestimable troupe, each with its novel arrangement of actual regulations, constants, and real factors.

One conspicuous adaptation of the multiverse hypothesis is the "many-universes understanding" of quantum mechanics. As per this understanding, each quantum occasion brings about the stretching of new universes, each addressing an alternate result of that occasion. Basically, the many-universes understanding places that a boundless number of equal real factors exist, continually expanding from our own with each quantum connection.

While the many-universes understanding remaining parts a subject of discussion among physicists and has not accomplished general acknowledgment, it addresses a captivating and mind-bowing thought that adjusts intimately with the idea of equal real factors investigated in sci-fi. The equal real factors in the many-universes translation are unique ideas as well as potential actual real factors that exist close by our own.

Equal real factors have likewise found their direction into the fields of quantum registering and computerized reasoning. Quantum registering, specifically, holds the commitment of recreating and investigating equal real factors. By bridling the standards of quantum mechanics, quantum PCs can perform computations that would be infeasible for old style PCs. These high level machines could be utilized to mimic quantum peculiarities and complex frameworks, possibly revealing insight into the idea of equal aspects and the secrets of the quantum world.

In the field of man-made brainpower, specialists are dealing with establishing virtual specialists and recreated conditions that can imitate human way of behaving and thought. These virtual creatures could exist in equal real factors inside the computerized domain, cooperating with people and adding to how we might interpret awareness and knowledge. The advancement of these virtual substances obscures the line among the real world and reproduction, offering new chances to investigate the idea of equal real factors.

The investigation of equal truths isn't restricted to the physical and advanced domains; it additionally reaches out into the domains of reasoning and mysticism. Logicians have long examined inquiries regarding the idea of the real world, presence, and the presence of numerous aspects or planes of being. The idea of equal real factors raises significant philosophical requests that challenge regular thoughts of truth, insight, and personality.

5.3 How these narratives influence societal views on reality

The stories that investigate equal universes and substitute real factors inside the sci-fi sort impact cultural perspectives on the real world. These accounts challenge how we might interpret what is genuine and open up conversations about the idea of truth, insight, and presence. They urge crowds to scrutinize the restrictions of their own existence and to think about the immense range of potential outcomes past our recognizable world. In this investigation of how these accounts impact cultural perspectives on the real world, we'll dive into different manners by which sci-fi has molded our aggregate comprehension of the world we live in.

Growing the Limits of Creative mind: Sci-fi stories highlighting equal universes act as a jungle gym for creative mind. They take us on excursions to universes where the laws of material science, nature, and rationale are unique in relation to our own. By introducing elective real factors, these accounts grow the limits of what is conceivable, empowering us to think imaginatively and imagine real factors past our ongoing comprehension. This development of creative mind encourages advancement and fills logical interest, prompting leap forwards in different fields.

Testing The customary way of thinking: Equal world accounts frequently challenge the standard way of thinking and business as usual. They request that we reevaluate our presumptions about the way the world works and the limits of our ongoing information. For instance, the many-universes understanding of quantum mechanics places that each quantum occasion brings about the making of new universes with various results. This thought difficulties how we might interpret circumstances and logical results, featuring the complicated and diverse nature of the real world.

Advancing Liberality: Sci-fi stories highlighting equal universes energize receptiveness and resistance. At the point when crowds experience various variants of the real world, they are provoked to think about the assorted viewpoints and convictions that exist in our own reality. This openness to elective perspectives can cultivate compassion and understanding, advancing a more comprehensive and tolerating society.

Scrutinizing the Idea of Truth: The idea of equal real factors brings up significant philosophical issues about the idea of truth. Assuming different equal universes exist, each with its own adaptation of occasions, it becomes testing to figure out what is dispassionately obvious. This difficulties the thought of a solitary, unadulterated fact of the matter and urges us to perceive that reality can be emotional, fluctuating starting with one reality then onto the next. This philosophical investigation welcomes us to ponder the idea of truth in our own lives.

Analyzing the Job of Insight: Equal world stories additionally dive into the way of thinking of discernment and epistemology. They brief us to scrutinize the unwavering quality of our faculties and the idea of discernment itself.

In the event that various real factors can coincide close by our own, each with its extraordinary arrangement of realities and encounters, it brings up issues about how we see and decipher our general surroundings. This assessment of insight urges us to consider the constraints of human information and the intricacies of the world as we see it.

Cultivating a Feeling of Marvel: Sci-fi stories highlighting equal universes move a feeling of miracle and interest. They welcome us to investigate the obscure and ponder the limitless conceivable outcomes of the universe. This feeling of marvel can be a strong inspiration for logical investigation and revelation, as it urges us to look for replies to questions that might lie past the limits of our ongoing reality.

Featuring the Butterfly Impact: Many equal world accounts delineate the idea of the butterfly impact, where little changes in a single reality can prompt immensely various results. This thought builds up the interconnectedness of occasions and activities in our own reality, stressing the significance of our decisions and their possible outcomes. It fills in as an update that our choices have expansive impacts, regardless of whether we may not quickly see them.

Investigating Moral Difficulties: Sci-fi stories frequently present moral problems connected with the control of the real world, time, or history. These difficulties brief conversations about the results of our activities and choices. By investigating the moral ramifications of messing with the past or modifying the direction of occasions, these accounts urge crowds to think about the ethical components of their own decisions.

Encouraging Decisive Reasoning: Equal world stories challenge crowds to think basically and think about the ramifications of various real factors. They welcome us to draw in with complex ideas and investigate the outcomes of different situations. This decisive reasoning reaches out past the domain of fiction, empowering people to move toward true issues with an additional logical and receptive point of view.

Empowering Advancement and Investigation: Sci-fi stories including equal universes frequently act as wellsprings of motivation for researchers, designers, and creators. These accounts present historic thoughts and ideas that can ignite development in different fields. For example, the idea of equal aspects has impacted research in quantum material science, quantum figuring, and computerized reasoning. The investigation of these logical boondocks is driven by the craving to push the limits of our insight and find additional opportunities.

Animating Discussion and Conversation: Equal world stories invigorate discussion and conversation among crowds. Watchers and perusers are urged to share their understandings and speculations about the tales, prompting connecting with discussions about the idea of the real world and the potential outcomes of equal aspects. These conversations can unite individuals, encouraging a feeling of local area and imparted interest to the unexplored world.

Motivating New Ages: Notorious sci-fi accounts including equal universes keep on rousing new ages of scholars, producers, researchers, and makers. The persevering through allure of these accounts guarantees that the investigation of equal real factors stays a dynamic and developing subject. As more youthful ages are acquainted with these accounts, they are urged to think basically, investigate the obscure, and add to the continuous discourse about the idea of the real world.

In rundown, sci-fi stories highlighting equal universes impact cultural perspectives on the real world. They extend the limits of creative mind, challenge the tried and true way of thinking, advance liberality, question the idea of truth, look at the job of insight, cultivate a feeling of marvel, feature the butterfly impact, investigate moral situations, and support decisive reasoning. These accounts likewise move development and investigation, animate discussion and conversation, and rouse new ages to contemplate the secrets of equal real factors. By introducing elective universes and testing how we might alterpret reality, these stories improve our social scene and urge us to embrace the huge range of potential outcomes past our own reality.

Chapter 6

Navigating Between Realities

Exploring between truths is a significant and complex idea that rises above the limits of our ordinary presence. In reality as we know it where innovation, science, and reasoning constantly push the limits of our comprehension, moving between various planes of reality takes on new importance. This excursion investigates the diverse idea of the real world, the manners by which we associate with and see it, and the significant ramifications that exploring between these various realities can have on our lives and the actual texture of our universe.

At its center, the idea of exploring between real factors difficulties our basic comprehension of what is genuine and what isn't. It questions the limits of our actual world and difficulties our impression of time, space, and presence. This investigation isn't restricted to the domain of sci-fi or the elusive, yet it addresses the actual embodiment of human experience.

One method for moving toward this idea is from the perspective of quantum mechanics, a field of physical science that has upset how we might interpret the subatomic world. In quantum mechanics, particles can exist in different states at the same time, a peculiarity known as superposition. It proposes that at the littlest sizes of the real world, the qualification between what is genuine and what isn't becomes obscured. This thought difficulties our traditional, Newtonian perspective on the world, where everything is conveniently characterized and unsurprising.

The idea of superposition isn't restricted to particles alone. It has been stretched out to envelop bigger frameworks, including the possibility that naturally visible articles, even whole universes, could exist in different states without a moment's delay. This prompts the idea of a multiverse, where incalculable universes coincide close by our own, each with its one of a kind arrangement of actual regulations and conditions. Exploring between these equal universes would require an extreme change in how we might interpret reality.

While the possibility of the multiverse is as yet a hypothetical idea, it features the significant intricacy of the real world and the potential for exploring between various realities. On the off chance that these equal universes exist, they could offer a brief look into a tremendous range of potential outcomes, each with its remarkable results and results. Exploring between these substitute real factors could open up a universe of neglected open doors and difficulties.

The thought of exploring between truths isn't restricted to the domain of science and physical science; it stretches out into the domains of cognizance and insight. Our view of the truth is profoundly impacted by our tangible encounters and the manner in which our cerebrums decipher the data they get. The mind goes about as a channel, handling a tremendous measure of tangible information and building our emotional reality. This development can be impacted by variables like culture, convictions, and individual encounters.

Brain research and neuroscience have revealed insight into the pliability of our discernment and the job it plays in forming our existence. Our minds can be profoundly versatile, and under specific circumstances, they can create modified conditions of cognizance. These modified states, whether prompted by reflection, stimulating substances, or different means, can prompt significant changes in discernment and, at times, a feeling of exploring between various real factors.

For instance, hallucinogenic encounters have been portrayed as excursions that take people to substitute domains of discernment and cognizance. These changed states can offer special bits of knowledge, sensations of interconnectedness, and a feeling of rising above the limits of common reality. While the specific instruments behind these encounters are as yet a subject of continuous examination, they feature the versatility of human cognizance and the potential for exploring between various perspectives.

Besides, the investigation of clear dreaming gives one more viewpoint on exploring between real factors. In a clear dream, the visionary becomes mindful that they are in a fantasy and can at times apply a level of command over the fantasy's story and climate. Clear dreams permit people to investigate and communicate with an alternate reality, one made completely by their own brain. These encounters can be extraordinary, offering a brief look into the inventive capability of our cognizance.

The idea of exploring between real factors additionally has profound philosophical ramifications. It challenges how we might interpret oneself and the idea of personality. On the off chance that we can exist in different conditions of the real world or cognizance, then, at that point, the idea of a solitary, perpetual self turns out to be less obvious. It brings up issues about the congruity of personality and whether our identity is a deception made by our restricted insight.

One philosophical way to deal with exploring between truths is established in the idea of modular authenticity. Modular authenticity proposes that all potential universes are similarly genuine, existing autonomously of our insight or experience. As per this view, exploring between truths doesn't involve making or annihilating universes yet rather moving our viewpoint to possess one of the many existing universes.

The logician David Lewis, a defender of modular authenticity, contended that the multiverse is definitely not a hypothetical develop yet a mystical reality. In this view, we are continually exploring between various universes, however we may not be deliberately mindful of it. Each decision we make, each choice, each second, drives us to various parts of the multiverse. While this understanding has its portion of cynics, it brings up fascinating issues about the idea of presence and the job of decision in exploring between real factors.

Past the domains of science, brain research, and reasoning, exploring between truths is an idea well established in mankind's set of experiences and culture. It tracks down articulation in fantasies, legends, and strict stories that portray excursions to supernatural domains, experiences with gods, and the investigation of adjusted conditions of cognizance. These accounts mirror mankind's getting through interest with rising above the limits of conventional reality.

In numerous native societies, the utilization of ceremonies and holy substances has been a way to explore between various conditions of cognizance. Shamanic rehearses, for instance, include entering modified states to speak with the soul world and gain bits of knowledge into the idea of the real world. These encounters are many times seen as a method for overcoming any barrier between the physical and otherworldly elements of presence.

Exploring between truths isn't restricted to old practices; it is likewise a focal subject in contemporary craftsmanship and writing. Oddity, for example, looks to upset the limits of the real world and make an illusory, unreasonable world that challenges our regular comprehension of the genuine. Craftsmen like Salvador Dali and René Magritte have investigated the territory between the cognizant and the inner mind, welcoming watchers to mull over the idea of reality itself.

Sci-fi writing and movies have for some time been a stage for investigating the idea of exploring between real factors. Works like Philip K. Dick's "The Man in the High Palace" and Christopher Nolan's "Commencement" dig into substitute aspects, equal universes, and the obscuring of the real world and deception. These accounts enamor our creative mind and incite us to consider the potential outcomes of exploring between various realities.

One of the most persevering and intriguing parts of exploring between truths is the potential effect it can have on our lives and our general surroundings. On the off chance that we could tackle the capacity to move between various conditions of the real world, what's the significance here for our self-awareness, connections, and comprehension of the universe?

One expected outcome of exploring between truths is the capacity to acquire new viewpoints and experiences. By encountering various realities, we might reveal answers for complex issues, access undiscovered innovativeness, and foster a more significant comprehension of ourselves and the world. This extraordinary potential isn't restricted to individual development yet could stretch out to more extensive cultural changes.

In the domain of science and innovation, the capacity to explore between real factors could prompt progressive headways. For instance, quantum processing, which depends on the standards of quantum superposition, holds the commitment of tackling complex issues that are presently past the span of old style PCs. On the off chance that we can outfit the force of superposition and quantum trap, it could prompt leap forwards in fields like cryptography, drug revelation, and man-made brainpower.

The clinical field additionally stands to profit from the idea of exploring between real factors. Changed conditions of awareness, whether instigated by contemplation or different means, have been related with worked on psychological wellness, decreased pressure, and improved prosperity. Helpful methodologies that include exploring between various conditions of awareness, like hallucinogenic helped treatment, are being investigated as expected medicines for different emotional well-being conditions, including gloom, tension, and post-horrible pressure issue.

The ramifications of exploring between real factors stretch out to how we might interpret time and the idea of causality. In a multiverse system, where endless equal universes coincide, the past, present, and future might assume an alternate personality. The idea of time travel, once consigned to the domain of sci-fi, could turn into a reality. Exploring between various time spans and interfacing with substitute adaptations of history could have extensive outcomes, bringing up issues about the morals and obligation related with such abilities.

Besides, the idea of exploring between real factors can possibly reshape how we might interpret the climate and the difficulties we face in the 21st 100 years. Environmental change, asset exhaustion, and ecological debasement are major problems that request inventive arrangements. Exploring between various conditions of reality could offer new points of view on these difficulties and move novel ways to deal with manageability, protection, and the conservation of our planet.

The moral contemplations encompassing exploring between truths are of principal significance. Similarly as with any strong innovation or capacity, the mindful utilization of such capacities is a basic concern. How would we guarantee that the potential for exploring between truths is utilized for everyone's benefit and doesn't prompt unseen side-effects or damage?

One critical part of moral route between truths is the safeguarding of individual independence and assent. For instance, with regards to remedial or clinical intercessions that include adjusted conditions of cognizance, it is fundamental to guarantee that people give informed assent and have organization over their encounters. Safeguarding weak populaces and forestalling pressure or control is critical.

In the domain of innovation, issues of protection and security come to the very front. Quantum registering and other trend setting innovations that influence the standards of superposition and ensnarement can possibly disturb current encryption techniques.

This raises worries about information security and the need to foster new shields to safeguard individual data and computerized resources in our current reality where exploring between real factors turns into a reality.

Also, exploring between real factors can have potentially negative results on the texture of our general public. The obscuring of the line among the real world and deception could lead to falsehood, disinformation, and the control of public insight. Guaranteeing the uprightness of data and shielding against the maltreatment of these capacities is a squeezing worry for states, establishments, and people the same.

The moral elements of exploring between real factors additionally reach out to natural and environmental contemplations. While the capacity to acquire new points of view on natural difficulties is important, it is basic that these experiences are utilized to advance supportability and safeguard the planet. Flippant utilization of this innovation could worsen natural debasement or lead to unanticipated environmental results.

As we ponder the moral components of exploring between real factors, obviously dependable administration and a hearty structure of regulations and guidelines will be vital. Society should wrestle with the difficulties and valuable open doors that this idea presents, cultivating an aggregate discourse to guarantee that the potential for exploring between truths is bridled to serve all.

Exploring between truths is an idea that challenges the actual groundworks of how we might interpret reality, cognizance, and presence. It incorporates many disciplines, from quantum material science to brain research, theory, and social customs. It addresses the potential for individual change, logical leap forwards, and cultural change. As we investigate this idea, we should wrestle with the moral contemplations that accompany it, guaranteeing that the dependable utilization of these abilities lines up with our qualities and the improvement of humankind.

All in all, exploring between truths is a significant and diverse idea that welcomes us to rethink the idea of the real world and our place inside it. Whether from the perspective of quantum mechanics, adjusted conditions of cognizance, reasoning, or social accounts, this idea moves us to rise above the restrictions of our ongoing comprehension. It holds the commitment of groundbreaking bits of knowledge, logical progressions, and inventive answers for probably the most major problems within recent memory. Notwithstanding, it likewise requests cautious thought of the moral ramifications and the dependable utilization of these capacities to defend our future and the world we possess. As we keep on investigating the conceivable outcomes of exploring between real factors, we set out on an excursion that could reshape the actual texture of our reality.

6.1 Theoretical concepts and devices for traversing parallel worlds

Hypothetical ideas and gadgets for navigating equal universes address an intriguing domain of logical request, pushing the limits of how we might interpret reality and the universe. These ideas, frequently investigated in the domains of hypothetical material science, speculative fiction, and philosophical talk, propose the presence of numerous equal universes close by our own, each with its extraordinary arrangement of actual regulations and conditions. While these ideas remain generally hypothetical, they charm the creative mind and have produced interesting thoughts regarding the idea of the real world and the potential for route between these substitute aspects.

One of the principal hypothetical structures for exploring between equal universes is the idea of the multiverse. The multiverse places that our universe is only one of many, existing inside an immense inestimable group of universes, each with its unmistakable properties and major constants. The possibility of the multiverse has gotten some decent momentum in ongoing many years, prodded by advancements in cosmology and quantum physical science.

With regards to cosmology, the inflationary multiverse speculation recommends that during the quick extension of the early universe, various areas might have formed into discrete "bubble" universes with their own actual qualities. These air pocket universes could possess various areas of spacetime, making them unavailable to each other inside our perceptible universe. Exploring between these air pocket universes would require a significant comprehension of the hidden cosmological cycles, which, at this stage, remains simply hypothetical.

Quantum mechanics likewise offers hypothetical ideas that converge with equal universes. The hypothesis of quantum superposition sets that particles can exist in numerous states all the while until noticed, testing our traditional, deterministic perspective on the real world. A few understandings of quantum mechanics, like the Many-Universes Translation (MWI), recommend that each quantum occasion makes a spreading of universes, bringing about a large number of equal real factors where each conceivable result happens.

In the MWI, exploring between these equal universes is an intrinsic outcome of quantum occasions. It suggests that each choice, regardless of how apparently irrelevant, brings about the formation of another universe, each comparing to an alternate decision or result. While the MWI has its portion of defenders and pundits, it highlights the potential for a practically limitless number of substitute real factors existing together close by our own.

Notwithstanding the hypothetical idea of these ideas, they have touched off a lot of hypothesis about the improvement of gadgets or strategies for crossing equal universes. Hypothetical conversations frequently base on the accompanying ideas and gadgets that could, on a fundamental level, empower such route:

Wormholes: Wormholes are hypothetical alternate routes through spacetime, interfacing far off districts or even various universes. In principle, navigating a wormhole could empower a type of interdimensional travel. Nonetheless, the presence of wormholes and the plausibility of crossing them stays speculative and is a subject of continuous logical examination.

Alcubierre Drive: The Alcubierre drive, otherwise called the "twist drive," is a hypothetical idea inside the system of general relativity. It hypothesizes the production of a twist bubble around a shuttle, successfully contracting spacetime before the vessel and growing it behind, taking into consideration quicker than-light travel. While the Alcubierre drive has been investigated in principle, critical difficulties, including the prerequisite for extraordinary matter with negative energy thickness, should be defeated for its reasonable acknowledgment.

Quantum Burrowing: Quantum burrowing is a peculiarity where particles, like electrons, can go through energy hindrances that traditional physical science would consider unfavorable. Hypothetically, quantum burrowing could take into consideration the entry between various quantum states or substitute real factors. Be that as it may, the control and consistency of such burrowing occasions stay subtle.

Fascinating Matter: Certain hypothetical ideas for interdimensional travel propose the utilization of outlandish matter with properties not tracked down in our universe. Colorful matter could be utilized to control spacetime and make the circumstances important for navigating between equal universes. The plausibility of creating and using fascinating matter remaining parts a critical test.

Quantum PCs: High level quantum PCs have been proposed as expected gadgets for exploring between equal universes. Quantum processing use the standards of quantum superposition and trap to perform computations that old style PCs can't. While quantum PCs can possibly reproduce quantum frameworks and possibly investigate substitute real factors, they are still in their outset and face significant specialized obstacles.

Cognizance and Brain Body Communication: A few philosophical and supernatural points of view recommend that the psyche assumes a critical part in exploring between equal universes. These perspectives set that cognizance, aim, or modified perspectives could work with the experience of various aspects. Such thoughts frequently cross with rehearses like contemplation, clear dreaming, and other changed conditions of cognizance.

String Hypothesis and the Scene: In the system of string hypothesis, there is an idea known as the "scene." The scene proposes the presence of a huge range of potential vacuum expresses, each comparing to an extraordinary arrangement of actual regulations and constants. Exploring between these different vacuum states inside string hypothesis could be viewed as a type of interdimensional travel. In any case, the pragmatic means to accomplish this route inside the scene stays a subject of hypothetical investigation.

These hypothetical ideas and gadgets offer a brief look into the different and creative manners by which mankind has considered exploring between equal universes. It means quite a bit to take note of that, as of now, these thoughts exist generally in the domain of hypothetical material science, speculative fiction, and philosophical request. The useful acknowledgment of such gadgets or techniques stays unsure and is much of the time compelled by our ongoing comprehension of the laws of material science.

One of the critical difficulties in investigating the hypothetical ideas for navigating equal universes is the absence of exploratory proof to help these thoughts. While hypothetical structures give an establishment to examining interdimensional travel, experimental approval is restricted. This has prompted an extensive hole between hypothetical hypothesis and commonsense acknowledgment.

One more test is the issue of energy necessities and the essential impediments forced by the laws of material science. A large number of the ideas, for example, wormholes and twist drives, require outlandish matter with properties that are not at present known to exist in our universe. The energy prerequisites for controlling spacetime in these ways might be past our mechanical capacities.

Moreover, the moral and philosophical ramifications of interdimensional travel ought to be considered carefully. The capacity to explore between equal universes brings up significant issues about private character, moral obligation, and the outcomes of our activities. It additionally presents the test of deciding how the information and abilities acquired from interdimensional travel ought to be shared and made due.

The quest for interdimensional travel is a charming subject in speculative fiction, where it has been investigated in endless books, movies, and TV series. These stories frequently mistreat the logical ideas, involving them as a background for convincing stories. They give a brief look into the human interest with the obscure and the longing to investigate unfamiliar domains, whether they exist in far off cosmic systems, substitute aspects, or equal universes.

In sci-fi, creators and producers frequently acquaint inventive gadgets and ideas with empower interdimensional travel, for example, gateways, time machines, and gadgets that control the texture of spacetime. These gadgets act as story apparatuses to investigate the results of exploring between equal universes and the effect on the characters and social orders included.

One exemplary illustration of interdimensional travel in sci-fi is H.G. Wells' novella "The Time Machine," in which a person who goes back and forth through time imagines a machine that permits him to travel through time, visiting the far off future and experiencing various forms of Earth. Wells' work has impacted endless different creators and producers, establishing time travel as a staple of sci-fi.

In mainstream society, the idea of equal universes and substitute truths is likewise conspicuous. The "multiverse" has turned into a common subject in superhuman comic books and transformations, with characters like The Blaze and Bug Man experiencing substitute variants of themselves in equal universes. These accounts investigate the idea that decisions and occasions in a single reality can make dissimilar results in others.

TV series like "Sliders" and "Periphery" have taken navigating equal universes as a focal reason, permitting characters to investigate and interface with substitute renditions of Earth. These shows dig into the moral and philosophical ramifications of interdimensional travel and the effect on the people in question.

Sci-fi's depiction of interdimensional travel frequently ignites discussions about the idea of the real world, decision, and the results of our activities. While these accounts might mistreat the logical subtleties, they urge crowds to consider the potential outcomes and constraints of exploring between equal universes.

6.2 Portals, wormholes, and alternate dimensions

Entries, wormholes, and substitute aspects address entrancing and frequently speculative ideas that have enamored the human creative mind for ages. These thoughts rise above the limits of regular physical science and welcome us to think about the chance of crossing between various domains, universes, or aspects. Whether tracked down in the domains of sci-fi, hypothetical physical science, or philosophical talk, these ideas bring up significant issues about the idea of room, time, and reality.

Perhaps of the most conspicuous and generally perceived idea in the domain of interdimensional travel is the possibility of entryways. Entries, otherwise called entryways or doors, are imagined as openings or paths that interface one area to another, frequently across immense distances or even various aspects. Entrances have been a repetitive subject in folklore, old stories, and sci-fi, catching the human interest with the obscure and the craving to investigate past the restrictions of our existence.

In antiquated folklore and fables, entryways are many times portrayed as otherworldly or mysterious passages that permit people to get to stowed away universes, domains of divine beings or powerful creatures, or even eternity. For instance, the Greek legend Orpheus is said to have utilized an entry, the Obscure Egg, to slip into the Hidden world in his mission to save his cherished Eurydice. In Norse folklore, the Bifrost Scaffold fills in as a rainbow-shaded gateway associating the domains of the divine beings and people.

With regards to sci-fi and dream writing, entryways are every now and again depicted as items or gadgets that empower characters to venture out momentarily to various areas or aspects. J.K. Rowling's "Harry Potter" series, for instance, presents the idea of Portkeys, common items that, when actuated, transport people to explicit objections.

Essentially, C.S. Lewis' "The Accounts of Narnia" highlights captivated closets that act as entryways to the otherworldly place that is known for Narnia.

While entrances are staples of old stories and fiction, they remain to a great extent the stuff of legend and dream in our ongoing comprehension of physical science. In logical terms, the possibility of entryways that can ship us across significant stretches or into substitute aspects is profoundly speculative and not upheld by experimental proof. By the by, physicists keep on investigating hypothetical ideas that might actually prompt a comprehension of such peculiarities.

One hypothetical idea connected with gateways is the thought of a navigable wormhole. Wormholes, otherwise called Einstein-Rosen spans, are theoretical entries through spacetime that could interface two far off focuses, possibly taking into account interdimensional travel. The idea of wormholes emerges from the situations of general relativity, Einstein's hypothesis of gravity, which depicts how enormous articles twist spacetime.

In a worked on perception, a wormhole can be envisioned as a passage or conductor with two closures, each arranged at various areas in spacetime. On the off chance that such a construction were to exist, it could offer an easy route for crossing huge vast distances or in any event, interfacing various aspects. The thought of wormholes has been advocated in sci-fi, with creators and producers frequently involving them as plot gadgets for interstellar travel and excursions to different domains.

Be that as it may, the hypothetical structure for wormholes is definitely more mind boggling and testing than fictitious depictions propose. Hypothetical physicists have distinguished a few huge deterrents to the presence of navigable wormholes, including issues connected with solidness, the prerequisite for fascinating matter, and the evasion of oddities related with time travel. Wormholes that don't fall under their own gravitational powers, and that can be explored without imperiling voyagers, remain simply hypothetical develops.

One of the critical difficulties in understanding the idea of wormholes is the prerequisite for outlandish matter, a speculative type of issue with negative energy thickness. Extraordinary matter would be expected to keep the wormhole open and forestall its prompt breakdown. The presence and properties of outlandish matter are still subjects of hypothesis and discussion inside mainstream researchers.

One more captivating part of wormholes is their capability to associate far off places in space as well as various moments. With regards to time travel, navigable wormholes could hypothetically give a way to get to the past or what's to come. Nonetheless, this idea presents significant oddities, for example, the renowned "granddad conundrum," where turning back the clock could prompt the chance of forestalling one's own reality.

The moral and philosophical ramifications of time travel through wormholes are huge. Inquiries concerning individual character, causality, and the effect of time travel on the past, present, and future have been subjects of profound philosophical investigation. While these contemplations add layers of intricacy to the idea of wormholes, they likewise make it an enrapturing subject for logical and philosophical request.

While navigable wormholes stay speculative, researchers keep on investigating the chance of their reality and the circumstances under which they may be made or bridled. In hypothetical physical science, the investigation of wormholes is progressing, with scientists exploring whether the laws of general relativity could consider the arrangement of steady and traversable wormholes.

Another hypothetical idea that crosses with substitute aspects and interdimensional travel is the Many-Universes Translation (MWI) of quantum mechanics. The MWI recommends that each quantum occasion with different potential results makes a fanning of the universe, bringing about the presence of innumerable equal real factors. In this translation, each decision, regardless of how little, brings about the making of another universe, each comparing to an alternate result.

The MWI raises the interesting chance of interdimensional travel by suggesting that there are a practically boundless number of substitute real factors coinciding close by our own. In principle, if a method for exploring between these equal real factors could be created, people could investigate the huge swath of potential results that emerge from various decisions and occasions.

Notwithstanding, the idea of exploring between equal universes in the MWI remains generally hypothetical and speculative. While the MWI is a genuine understanding of quantum mechanics, it has not been observationally affirmed, and the method for getting to these equal truths are not illustrated inside the structure of the actual translation.

In addition, the moral and philosophical ramifications of the MWI are significant. The possibility that each decision and occasion prompts the formation of new real factors brings up issues about private personality, the idea of freedom of thought, and the results of our activities. It challenges how we might interpret causality and determinism, featuring the intricacy of exploring between equal universes in a multiverse characterized by quantum expanding.

Past the domains of hypothetical physical science, substitute aspects and interdimensional travel has been a focal topic in sci-fi and speculative writing. Creators and producers have utilized these ideas to investigate the human longing to rise above the restrictions of our existence and to wrestle with inquiries regarding personality, decision, and the results of our activities.

The idea of substitute aspects is a typical topic in sci-fi writing and has been promoted in works like H.G. Wells' "The Time Machine." In Wells' novel, the hero concocts a time machine that permits him to go through time and investigate various variants of Earth in the far off future. This investigation of substitute aspects gives a structure to considering the outcomes of cultural decisions and individual activities.

Essentially, the idea of substitute aspects is a focal subject in Philip K. Dick's book "The Man in the High Palace," which presents an other history where the Pivot powers won The Second Great War. The story investigates how various decisions and results can prompt completely disparate real factors, inciting perusers to think about the delicacy of authentic occasions and the potential for interdimensional travel.

In film and TV, substitute aspects has been a common theme in establishments like "A Twilight Zone," "Periphery," and "More odd Things." These accounts frequently portray characters who coincidentally end up in equal universes, where the laws of material science, society, or ethical quality vary from their own. The investigation of these other aspects fills in as a vehicle for investigating the intricacies of human life and the results of our choices.

Likewise with wormholes and gateways, the depiction of substitute aspects in sci-fi offers an imaginative focal point through which to look at the human condition. These stories urge watchers and perusers to ponder the likely repercussions of decisions and activities, featuring the interconnectedness of occasions and the different potential outcomes that exist inside the multiverse.

Hypothetical ideas and gadgets for navigating equal universes, including entrances, wormholes, and substitute aspects, keep on being subjects of interest and interest. These thoughts catch the human creative mind, starting philosophical, moral, and logical conversations about the idea of the real world and the chance of interdimensional travel.

At their center, these ideas challenge our customary comprehension of room, time, and causality. They bring up significant issues about the attainability of getting to various domains or aspects and the outcomes of such travel. The moral and philosophical ramifications of interdimensional travel are critical, welcoming us to ponder issues.

6.3 The challenges and consequences of interdimensional travel

Interdimensional travel, an idea that has long caught the human creative mind through sci-fi, hypothetical physical science, and philosophical hypothesis, presents a bunch of difficulties and outcomes that rise above the domains of fiction and dream. While venturing between substitute aspects, equal universes, or various planes of the truth is an alluring and intriguing idea, it is fundamental to think about the intricacies, both down to earth and hypothetical, related with so much travel, as well as the significant ramifications it conveys for how we might interpret the universe and our place inside it.

One of the most basic difficulties of interdimensional travel is established in the hypothetical and logical establishments whereupon such ideas are assembled. The actual presence of substitute aspects, equal universes, or interdimensional gateways stays speculative and doubtful by experimental proof. While hypothetical material science gives structures to investigating these thoughts, for example, the idea of the multiverse, these thoughts frequently lie beyond our ongoing logical comprehension.

Hypothetical physical science has presented captivating ideas, like navigable wormholes and the Many-Universes Understanding (MWI) of quantum mechanics, which propose the potential for interdimensional travel. Wormholes, for example, are speculative entries through spacetime, while the MWI sets the presence of incalculable equal real factors. Nonetheless, these hypotheses are overflowing with hypothetical and useful snags.

One of the vital difficulties in the hypothetical acknowledgment of interdimensional travel is the prerequisite for fascinating matter, a speculative type of issue with negative energy thickness. Colorful matter would be important to balance out wormholes and forestall their prompt breakdown. The presence and properties of colorful matter stay speculative, and it is hazy whether such matter can be produced or tackled from a functional perspective.

Besides, the thought of interdimensional travel brings up moral and philosophical issues about the idea of the real world and character. On the off chance that other aspects exist, how would they influence our healthy identity and individual character? What are the outcomes of exploring between various aspects, and how can it impact the course of one's life and their decisions? These inquiries welcome thought of the connection between our decisions, our activities, and the texture of the multiverse.

Interdimensional travel is additionally intently attached to the idea of time travel. Numerous hypothetical models for interdimensional travel, like wormholes, make the way for the chance of moving between various areas as well as between various moments. This convergence of existence adds a layer of intricacy to the difficulties and outcomes of interdimensional travel.

The potential for time travel presents Catch 22s, for example, the "granddad oddity," in which a person who jumps through time could modify the past in a manner that forestalls their own reality. The moral and philosophical ramifications of time travel are significant, bringing up issues about causality, choice, and the ethical obligation of people who have the capacity to control time.

Additionally, interdimensional travel and time travel ideas challenge how we might interpret causality and determinism. They recommend that what's to come isn't permanently established, and that occasions and decisions can prompt various results. This view difficulties the old style Newtonian perspective, where the universe works under severe determinism, with each impact having an unmistakable and recognizable reason.

One more test related with interdimensional travel is the issue of energy necessities and the central constraints forced by the laws of physical science. Ideas like wormholes and twist drives frequently require colossal measures of energy and the presence of outlandish matter, the two of which stay hypothetical builds. The reasonable acknowledgment of these innovations is a long ways past our ongoing mechanical capacities.

In the domain of time travel, hypothetical models frequently require the capacity to control spacetime itself, which brings up issues about the practicality of such controls and the energy prerequisites they would involve. The energy challenges related with interdimensional and time travel stay huge hindrances.

The moral contemplations encompassing interdimensional travel are fundamental. The possibility to explore between various aspects, whether through entrances, wormholes, or different means, conveys critical moral ramifications. These contemplations include issues of individual independence, assent, and the obligations related with having interdimensional travel abilities.

For example, with regards to restorative or clinical intercessions that include interdimensional travel, guaranteeing that people give informed assent and have office over their encounters is pivotal. Safeguarding weak populaces and forestalling compulsion or control are fundamental moral contemplations in the turn of events and utilization of interdimensional travel advancements.

The dependable utilization of interdimensional venture out innovations stretches out to issues of protection and security. Progressed interdimensional travel strategies, like wormholes or quantum gateways, could have suggestions for information security and data insurance. Guaranteeing the protection of people and shielding against the abuse of these innovations is a critical moral concern.

Interdimensional travel advancements could likewise raise worries about the potential for falsehood and the control of public insight. The capacity to explore between various aspects could present open doors for duplicity and the mutilation of data. Safeguarding the trustworthiness of data and relieving the dangers of deception is a basic part of the moral difficulties related with interdimensional travel.

The outcomes of interdimensional travel, both at the individual and cultural levels, are significant and boundless. At a singular level, the capacity to explore between aspects could offer extraordinary bits of knowledge, encounters, and self-improvement potential open doors. It might prompt a more significant comprehension of oneself, individual personality, and the interconnectedness of one's decisions with the texture of the multiverse.

Helpful uses of interdimensional travel are another likely outcome. Changed conditions of cognizance, whether instigated by interdimensional travel strategies or different means, have been related with worked on emotional well-being, diminished pressure, and upgraded prosperity. Restorative methodologies that include exploring between various conditions of awareness, like hallucinogenic helped treatment, are being investigated as expected medicines for different emotional wellness conditions, including discouragement, uneasiness, and post-horrible pressure issue.

The expected cultural results of interdimensional travel are tremendous and interconnected with the moral contemplations encompassing the innovation. In the domain of science and innovation, the capacity to explore between aspects could prompt progressive headways. Quantum processing, for instance, holds the commitment of taking care of mind boggling issues that are right now past the compass of old style PCs. In the event that we can bridle the force of interdimensional travel standards and quantum trap, it could prompt forward leaps in fields like cryptography, drug disclosure, and man-made reasoning.

The clinical field additionally stands to profit from the idea of interdimensional travel. Changed conditions of cognizance, whether instigated by interdimensional travel strategies or different means, have been related with worked on emotional well-being, decreased pressure, and upgraded prosperity. Remedial methodologies that include exploring between various conditions of awareness, like hallucinogenic helped treatment, are being investigated as expected medicines for different psychological wellness conditions, including sadness, nervousness, and post-horrible pressure issue.

The ramifications of interdimensional head out stretch out to how we might interpret the climate and the difficulties we face in the 21st 100 years. Environmental change, asset consumption, and ecological corruption are major problems that request inventive arrangements. Interdimensional travel could offer new viewpoints on these difficulties and move novel ways to deal with supportability, protection, and the conservation of our planet.

One of the most persevering and captivating parts of interdimensional travel is the potential effect it can have on our lives and our general surroundings. In the event that we could outfit the capacity to move between various aspects, what's the significance here for our self-awareness, connections, and comprehension of the universe?

The dependable utilization of interdimensional travel innovations is a basic concern. Likewise with any strong innovation or capacity, guaranteeing the dependable utilization of such capacities is of principal significance. How would we guarantee that the potential for interdimensional travel is utilized for everyone's best interests and doesn't prompt unseen side-effects or mischief?

One critical part of moral interdimensional travel is the conservation of individual independence and assent. With regards to restorative or clinical mediations that include interdimensional travel, it is fundamental to guarantee that people give informed assent and have office over their encounters. Safeguarding weak populaces and forestalling pressure or control is extremely critical.

In the domain of innovation, issues of protection and security come to the front. Quantum processing and other cutting edge innovations that influence the standards of superposition and entrapment can possibly disturb current encryption strategies.

Chapter 7

What If Scenarios

"Consider the possibility that" situations address an interesting and frequently speculative domain of human idea and request. These situations welcome us to investigate substitute real factors, think about the results of various decisions, and challenge how we might interpret circumstances and logical results. They assume a crucial part in different fields, including sci-fi, reasoning, direction, and logical request, and can go from the everyday to the unprecedented. These situations dazzle our minds, motivate imaginative reasoning, and urge us to consider the huge swath of potential outcomes that life and the universe could offer.

In the domain of logical request and trial and error, "consider the possibility that" situations act as basic devices for speculation testing and examination plan. Researchers frequently suggest speculative conversation starters to investigate potential results and decide the best ways of testing their hypotheses. By considering different "consider the possibility that" situations, analysts can distinguish likely factors, factors, and techniques that might yield important experiences. In fields like science, physical science, and brain research, these situations guide the advancement of tests and assist with molding the course of logical examination.

One eminent illustration of the utilization of "consider the possibility that" situations in logical request is the psychological test. Psychological tests are hypothetical situations that researchers and thinkers make to investigate perplexing and conceptual ideas. These situations permit analysts to inspect the outcomes of various premises and presumptions. Renowned models incorporate Albert Einstein's representations of riding close by a light emission to foster his hypothesis of unique relativity, and Erwin Schrödinger's fanciful feline to show the conundrum of quantum superposition.

In direction and critical thinking, "consider the possibility that" situations assume a focal part in system improvement and hazard evaluation. By taking into account a scope of potential results and reactions, people and associations can settle on additional educated choices and plan for possibilities. This training is especially significant in fields like money, where situation examination is utilized to survey the expected effect of different monetary, market, and international turns of events.

In day to day existence, individuals use "consider the possibility that" situations to explore a great many circumstances. For example, prior to settling on a critical important decision, people might ask themselves, "Consider the possibility that I seek after this vocation way?" or "Consider the possibility that I decide to concentrate abroad?" These situations assist people with weighing expected results, assess dangers, and imagine how their choices could mold their lives.

In writing, "consider the possibility that" situations are a foundation of sci-fi and speculative fiction. Creators in these classifications frequently suggest conversation starters like "Consider the possibility that people could go through time?" or "Imagine a scenario where we experienced extraterrestrial life?" to build creative stories that investigate the ramifications of such situations. These accounts offer perusers the valuable chance to ponder the results of logical headways, cultural changes, and the connection of mankind with different creatures and universes.

One notable illustration of "consider the possibility that" situations in writing is H.G. Wells' book "The Conflict of the Universes," which contemplates the situation of Earth being attacked by mechanically progressed Martians. The story fills in as a reflection on human weakness and versatility when stood up to with a profoundly progressed outsider civilization. Also, Philip K. Dick's "The Man in the High Palace" investigates an other history situation where the Pivot powers won The Second Great War, bringing up issues about the impact of verifiable occasions and the delicacy of the real world.

In mainstream society, "consider the possibility that" situations are fundamental to the idea of substitute real factors and equal universes. The possibility of various aspects or equal universes offers a material for investigating innumerable "imagine a scenario in which" situations. Whether it's the idea of a mirror universe in the "Star Trip" establishment or the "multiverse" in superhuman comics, these situations give a stage to narrating and looking at the results of disparate decisions and occasions.

For example, in the Wonder True to life Universe, the idea of the multiverse is key to the account. The film "Specialist Unusual" presents spreading real factors and the significance of safeguarding the strength of the multiverse. This idea makes ready for future storylines in what characters explore substitute aspects and equal universes, bringing "consider the possibility that" situations to life on the big screen.

In philosophical talk, "imagine a scenario in which" situations act as vehicles for investigating psychological studies that test crucial inquiries regarding presence, profound quality, and the idea of the real world. These situations urge savants to scrutinize their suppositions, challenge their convictions, and dive into the intricacies of moral issues. Psychological studies like the "streetcar issue" and the "Boat of Theseus" brief savants to consider how they would act in speculative circumstances and what standards guide their direction.

The "streetcar issue," for instance, presents a situation in which an individual should choose whether to redirect an out of control streetcar that would somehow hurt various people. The psychological study features the strain between utilitarian morals, which focus on everyone's benefit, and deontological morals, which stress adherence to moral standards. By inspecting such situations, scholars intend to acquire a more profound comprehension of moral and moral navigation.

In the domain of innovation, "consider the possibility that" situations assume an imperative part in development and hazard evaluation. Specialists and creators utilize these situations to think about possible disappointments, weaknesses, and wellbeing measures while growing new items and frameworks. Through "consider the possibility that" examination, they can recognize shortcomings, expect issues, and devise answers for guarantee the dependability and security of their manifestations.

An exemplary illustration of "consider the possibility that" situations in innovation is in the field of advanced plane design. While planning shuttle, engineers should represent an extensive variety of "consider the possibility that" situations, including gear glitches, gravitational powers, and the difficulties of reemergence into Earth's environment. These situations drive the advancement of frameworks and conventions to guarantee the wellbeing of space travelers and the progress of missions.

In the realm of money, "consider the possibility that" situations are key to gamble with the executives and venture techniques. Examiners and portfolio directors utilize situation examination to evaluate the likely effect of different monetary, market, and international advancements on speculations and monetary business sectors. These situations assist financial backers with planning for various results and settle on informed choices to moderate gamble and expand returns.

One of the most broadly perceived instances of "consider the possibility that" situations in finance is pressure trying, in which establishments evaluate how their monetary positions would passage under serious financial circumstances. These tests help banks, insurance agency, and other monetary establishments assess their strength and guarantee that they can endure financial shocks and emergencies.

With regards to environmental change and ecological manageability, "consider the possibility that" situations are vital to figuring out the likely results of various activities and arrangements. Environment models, for example, use "consider the possibility that" situations to reenact the effect of different ozone harming substance emanations levels and temperature changes in the world. These situations illuminate environment approaches and systems for alleviating the impacts of environmental change.

Situation arranging in business and vital administration is another space where "consider the possibility that" situations assume a critical part. Associations utilize situation intending to expect future turns of events, assess vital choices, and get ready for different possibilities. By considering numerous "imagine a scenario where" situations, organizations can adjust to evolving conditions, settle on additional educated choices, and foster strong methodologies that address a scope of conceivable outcomes.

One eminent illustration of situation arranging is Shell's utilization of the procedure during the 1970s. The oil organization utilized situation wanting to plan for different energy fates, including potential oil deficiencies and the effect of ecological worries. This approach permitted Shell to adjust its procedures and broaden its ventures, at last upgrading its versatility and intensity.

In medical care and clinical exploration, "consider the possibility that" situations are instrumental in looking at the expected impacts of sicknesses, therapies, and general wellbeing measures. Disease transmission experts use displaying and situation investigation to extend the course of irresistible infections and evaluate the effect of intercessions, for example, inoculation missions and social separating measures. These situations guide general wellbeing methodologies and readiness endeavors.

One of the most noticeable ongoing instances of "consider the possibility that" situations in medical services is the utilization of models to figure the spread of Coronavirus and survey the impacts of different control measures. Disease transmission specialists and general wellbeing specialists have utilized situation examination to expect medical services framework requests, assess the adequacy of immunization missions, and guide chiefs in answering the pandemic.

In the domain of global relations and discretion, "consider the possibility that" situations are key to vital preparation and compromise. Policymakers and negotiators consider different situations to expect international turns of events and evaluate likely results. By analyzing these situations, they can plan international strategies, arrange arrangements, and explore complex worldwide relations really.

One persevering through illustration of "consider the possibility that" situations in global relations is the Virus War and the idea of "commonly guaranteed obliteration" (Frantic). During the Virus War, both the US and the Soviet Association had enormous munititions stockpiles of atomic weapons. The "imagine a scenario in which" situation of an atomic clash highlighted the overwhelming outcomes that would result from such a contention, at last filling in as an impediment against the utilization of atomic weapons.

In training, "consider the possibility that" situations offer significant devices for improving decisive reasoning and critical thinking abilities. Teachers utilize speculative situations to draw in understudies, advance imaginative reasoning, and urge them to think about a scope of potential results. These situations cultivate scholarly interest and assist understudies with fostering the ability to assess decisions and outcomes.

An exemplary instructive illustration of "consider the possibility that" situations is moral quandaries introduced as contextual investigations. Understudies are approached to examine complex circumstances and propose arrangements while thinking about the moral ramifications of their decisions. These situations assist people with fostering their moral thinking and moral judgment.

In self-awareness and personal growth, "consider the possibility that" situations act as integral assets for defining objectives and imagining wanted results. People frequently ask themselves inquiries like "Consider the possibility that I accomplish the most amazing job I could ever ask for?" or "Consider the possibility that I accomplish my wellness objectives?" to rouse inspiration and plan for self-awareness. By taking into account these situations, individuals can imagine their goals and foster activity intends to accomplish them.

The idea of "consider the possibility that" situations can likewise be applied to history, offering a method for rethinking previous occasions and grasp their outcomes according to alternate points of view. Counterfactual history, or "elective history," suggests conversation starters like "Consider the possibility that a verifiable situation had transpired in an unexpected way?" By looking at substitute verifiable situations, antiquarians can acquire experiences into the meaning of key occasions and their part in forming the course of history.

One prominent illustration of counterfactual history is the subject of what could have occurred assuming specific death endeavors had succeeded. For example, "Consider the possibility that Archduke Franz Ferdinand had not been killed in Sarajevo in 1914?" This psychological test welcomes antiquarians to investigate how different authentic results might have adjusted the direction of The Second Great War and the ensuing course of history.

All in all, "consider the possibility that" situations are a flexible and useful asset for investigation, request, and imaginative reasoning across many fields and teaches. They permit us to examine the outcomes of various decisions, challenge our suspicions, and imagine a huge number of potential outcomes. "Consider the possibility that" situations act as a main impetus for logical disclosure, philosophical request, key preparation, and self-awareness. They are a demonstration of the force of human creative mind and our ability to investigate the unknown region representing things to come. As we keep on suggesting speculative conversation starters and investigate the likely results of various situations, we leave on an excursion of scholarly disclosure and self-reflection, uncovering the complexities of our reality and the vast potential outcomes it holds.

7.1 Exploring alternate histories and alternative outcomes

Human interest exceeds all logical limitations, and one of the most dazzling roads of our curiosity lies in investigating substitute accounts and elective results. These scholarly excursions take us past the domain of laid out realities and reported occasions, permitting us to imagine what could have happened had history followed an alternate way. As we dive into the theoretical "imagine a scenario in which" situations, we cross the halls of hypothesis and uncover a large number of potential outcomes that shed light on the intricacies of causality, human organization, and the complexities of the past.

The charm of substitute accounts has endured all through human progress, frequently appearing as counterfactual or elective history stories. These stories offer a new point of view on notable verifiable occasions and challenge our impression of verifiable determinism. By suggesting conversation starters, for example, "Imagine a scenario in which key verifiable situation had transpired in an unexpected way?" or "Consider the possibility that urgent figures had gone with elective choices?" elective history scholars make rich and creative stories that investigate the results of these modified directions of history.

One conspicuous illustration of substitute history is Philip K. Dick's "The Man in the High Palace," which imagines an existence where the Hub powers won The Second Great War. The original dives perusers into a reality where the US is separated into Japanese and Nazi-involved domains, offering an obvious takeoff from the verifiable record. This intriguing account prompts perusers to ponder the impact of verifiable occasions and the delicacy of reality itself.

Counterfactual history isn't bound to the domain of writing; it likewise fills in as a significant device for antiquarians. Students of history utilize elective history for the purpose of rethinking the meaning of key occasions and their effect on the course of history. By suggesting conversation starters like "Imagine a scenario where the death of Archduke Franz Ferdinand had not happened in 1914?" or "Imagine a scenario in which the Cuban Rocket Emergency had heightened to atomic conflict?" students of history can break down the elements that molded these urgent minutes and investigate the scope of possible results.

In the field of political theory, "consider the possibility that" situations offer experiences into the complexities of worldwide relations and tact. Negotiators and policymakers frequently take part in situation arranging, a training that includes imagining various expected international turns of events and their results. This approach permits them to figure out international strategies, arrange peaceful accords, and plan for a scope of possibilities. By considering unique "imagine a scenario in which" situations, they can settle on informed choices and explore the mind boggling scene of worldwide governmental issues.

The Virus War period fills in as an eminent illustration of the use of "consider the possibility that" situations in worldwide relations. During the Virus War, both the US and the Soviet Association had immense armories of atomic weapons. The speculative "consider the possibility that" situation of an atomic clash highlighted the horrendous outcomes that would result from such a contention, eventually filling in as a strong obstruction against the utilization of atomic weapons. This shared comprehension of the potential demolition related with atomic conflict assumed a crucial part in keeping up with the uncomfortable tranquility of the Virus War time.

In the field of logical request and trial and error, "consider the possibility that" situations are basic apparatuses for speculation testing and exploration plan. Researchers frequently utilize speculative inquiries to investigate potential results and shape their examination techniques.

By considering different "imagine a scenario in which" situations, specialists can recognize expected factors, refine their speculations, and foster tests that yield important experiences. These situations guide examinations in fields like science, physical science, and brain research, giving an establishment to the investigation of perplexing and conceptual ideas.

Psychological studies are an exemplary illustration of "consider the possibility that" situations in logical request. These hypothetical situations are made by researchers and rationalists to look at conceptual ideas and complex peculiarities. Psychological tests permit specialists to investigate the results of various premises and suspicions. One of the most well known models is Albert Einstein's representation of riding close by a light emission to foster his hypothesis of unique relativity. These situations act as scholarly jungle gyms where researchers can challenge their presumptions, suggest new conversation starters, and gain a more profound comprehension of the peculiarities they study.

In innovation and designing, "consider the possibility that" situations are vital to advancement and chance evaluation. Specialists and creators use these situations to think about expected disappointments, weaknesses, and wellbeing measures while growing new items and frameworks. By looking at different "consider the possibility that" situations, they can distinguish shortcomings, expect issues, and devise arrangements that guarantee the dependability and security of their manifestations.

Aeronautic design gives an exemplary illustration of "consider the possibility that" situations in innovation. While planning shuttle, engineers should represent a scope of speculative situations, including hardware glitches, gravitational powers, and the difficulties of reemergence into Earth's climate. These situations drive the improvement of frameworks and conventions that ensure the wellbeing of space travelers and the outcome of missions.

In navigation and critical thinking, "consider the possibility that" situations are significant for procedure improvement and hazard appraisal. People and associations utilize these situations to consider a range of potential results and devise alternate courses of action. By weighing different "consider the possibility that" situations, they can settle on informed choices, plan for possibilities, and explore complex difficulties actually. In finance, for example, situation examination is utilized to evaluate the expected effect of various monetary, market, and international advancements on speculations and monetary business sectors.

In daily existence, individuals use "consider the possibility that" situations to explore a large number of circumstances and choices. Prior to going with huge decisions, people frequently ask themselves inquiries like "Consider the possibility that I seek after this vocation way?" or "Imagine a scenario in which I decide to concentrate abroad?" These situations assist people with weighing expected results, assess dangers, and imagine how their choices could mold their lives. They give a structure to consideration and vital preparation, empowering people to settle on decisions that line up with their qualities and desires.

In self-awareness and personal growth, "consider the possibility that" situations assume a significant part in putting forth objectives and imagining wanted results. People utilize these situations to spur themselves, rouse self-awareness, and diagram a way toward their desires. By taking into account "consider the possibility that" situations like "Imagine a scenario in which I accomplish a truly amazing job?" or "Imagine a scenario in which I accomplish my wellness objectives?" people can make activity designs that lead to personal development and the acknowledgment of their yearnings.

In writing, "consider the possibility that" situations are a foundation of sci-fi and speculative fiction. Creators in these kinds frequently suggest conversation starters like "Consider the possibility that people could go through time?" or "Imagine a scenario in which we experienced extraterrestrial life?" to make innovative stories that investigate the ramifications of such situations. These accounts offer perusers the chance to examine the outcomes of logical headways, cultural changes, and humankind's cooperation with different creatures and universes.

One notable illustration of "consider the possibility that" situations in writing is H.G. Wells' "The Conflict of the Universes." The clever imagines a world where Earth is attacked by mechanically progressed Martians. This provocative story considers human weakness and flexibility when defied with a profoundly progressed outsider development. Likewise, Philip K. Dick's "The Man in the High Palace" investigates a substitute history wherein the Pivot powers won The Second Great War, bringing up issues about the impact of verifiable occasions and the delicacy of the real world.

7.2 Imagining how the world might be different in parallel realities

The idea of equal real factors, frequently connected with the multiverse speculation, is an interesting and mind-bowing thought that has caught the human creative mind for quite a long time. It proposes the presence of various universes or aspects that coincide close by our own, each with its own arrangement of actual regulations, occasions, and potential outcomes. This idea welcomes us to mull over how the world may be different in these equal real factors and makes the way for a domain of speculative investigation and imaginative idea.

At the core of the idea of equal real factors lies that each choice, activity, and occasion could prompt various different results. This idea challenges our customary comprehension of a direct and solitary reality, where situation unfurl in a foreordained succession. All things considered, it suggests that each decision and occasion could prompt an expanding of real factors, making a huge and interconnected multiverse of potential outcomes.

One of the most interesting parts of considering equal truths is the possibility of boundless variety. In a multiverse, each possible variety of reality might exist, from unobtrusive contrasts in our day to day routines to significant shifts in the direction of history and the laws of physical science themselves. This thought prompts us to envision how the world may be different in these substitute aspects.

In these equal real factors, one can envision an existence where verifiable occasions went off in strange directions. For instance, "consider the possibility that" situations like "Imagine a scenario in which the Roman Domain never fell?" or "Imagine a scenario in which the Modern Unrest happened in old China?" permit us to imagine tremendously unique social, political, and mechanical scenes. Such situations offer an enamoring look into how the world may be unique on the off chance that essential crossroads in history had unfurled in elective ways.

In an equal reality where the Roman Domain never fell, the Western world could have seen a consistent and solid tradition of Roman administration, culture, and impact. The ensuing improvement of science, innovation, and workmanship could have followed an unmistakable direction, with suggestions for the worldwide overall influence and the state of world civic establishments.

Likewise, in reality as we know it where the Modern Transformation happened in antiquated China, the course of mechanical headway and worldwide exchange might have been significantly changed. China could have arisen as a modern superpower, forming the cutting edge world in a novel and groundbreaking way. The outcomes of such a situation reach out to financial frameworks, international elements, and social trades.

The idea of equal real factors additionally welcomes us to think about the job of individual decisions and the "butterfly impact" in molding various universes. The butterfly impact recommends that little starting changes can prompt critical downstream outcomes. In equal real factors, these minor adjustments in choices and activities can swell outward to make completely various results.

Envision a reality where a verifiable figure went with various decisions. For example, "Consider the possibility that Abraham Lincoln had not sought after a political vocation?" Such a situation could prompt a substitute reality in which the American Nationwide conflict unfurled in an unexpected way, modifying the destiny of the US and the worldwide scene. The exchange between individual organization and verifiable occasions is a spellbinding part of thinking about how the world may be different in equal real factors.

In addition, the laws of material science themselves might differ in these equal real factors. The constants and major powers that administer our universe could take on various qualities, prompting different actual real factors. Hypothesizing about such varieties prompts questions like "Imagine a scenario in which gravity were more vulnerable?" or "Consider the possibility that the speed of light were unique."

In this present reality where gravity is more fragile, the consequences for heavenly bodies, the construction of systems, and the development of life itself could be decisively unmistakable. The actual texture of the real world, insofar as we can tell, would be changed. In like manner, changes in the speed of light could reshape the idea of causality, time, and the conceivable outcomes of interstellar travel.

The idea of equal real factors additionally reaches out to inquiries concerning the presence of extraterrestrial life. In an immense multiverse, it becomes conceivable to contrastingly imagine universes where shrewd life has developed. The circumstances forever, the structures it takes, and the potential for interstellar correspondence might change generally in these equal real factors.

In one equal reality, life might have emerged on a planet with drastically unique ecological circumstances, bringing about living beings with remarkable variations and capacities. In another, clever civic establishments could have created elective methods of correspondence and travel, connecting with them a mind boggling and fascinating undertaking.

One of the persevering through questions related with equal truths is the idea of the "reflect universe." Promoted in sci-fi, the mirror universe is an other reality that is a dull or contorted impression of our own. In this situation, recognizable characters and substances exist in an equal reality with differentiating virtues, inspirations, and results.

The idea of the mirror universe brings up provocative issues about human instinct, profound quality, and the job of decision in molding our fates. It prompts us to investigate how different moral and social structures could prompt drastically unique cultural standards and ways of behaving. This investigation can act as a mirror to our own reality, empowering us to reconsider our qualities and think about the effect of our decisions.

In writing and mainstream society, the idea of the multiverse and equal real factors has led to endless imaginative stories. Sci-fi creators and movie producers frequently utilize these thoughts as a material for narrating and investigation. They make substitute universes and situations to inspect the results of various decisions, mechanical headways, and cultural designs.

A great representation of this is the "Star Trip" establishment, which presented the idea of a mirror universe in a few of its series. In this equal reality, recognizable characters take on adjusted jobs and moral arrangements. This story gadget offers watchers an enamoring point of view because of decisions and moral choices on the course of history and individual predeterminations.

Likewise, the "Many-Universes Translation" (MWI) of quantum mechanics recommends that each conceivable result of a quantum occasion exists in a different part of the multiverse. This understanding has roused provocative works of fiction that investigate the ramifications of this thought. The film "Sliding Entryways" presents two equal real factors in view of a straightforward second in time, demonstrating the way that little choices can prompt unfathomably different life directions.

The idea of equal real factors likewise assumes a huge part in the hero kind. Comics and movies frequently highlight substitute aspects or universes in which notable characters have disparate foundations, capacities, and moral compasses. These stories challenge watchers and perusers to consider how various conditions can shape the characters and activities of these notorious figures.

In philosophical talk, the idea of equal real factors brings up significant issues about private personality, choice, and the idea of the real world. Savants participate in psychological studies to investigate these inquiries, presenting situations like "Imagine a scenario in which individual personality were not constant over the long haul?" or "Consider the possibility that through and through freedom were a deception."

In an equal reality where individual character isn't persistent over the long run, the thought of a constant self that endures from birth to death may be supplanted by a divided or liquid feeling of personality. This situation challenges how we might interpret oneself and brings up issues about the idea of memory, cognizance, and the idea of "I."

The possibility that freedom of thought may be a deception prompts inquiries regarding the idea of decision and organization. In reality as we know it where each choice and activity is foreordained, the idea of moral obligation and individual responsibility might take on new aspects. This situation welcomes us to mull over the ramifications of residing in a reality where our decisions are not genuinely our own.

The idea of equal real factors has likewise tracked down a spot in the domain of quantum material science, where it is related with the MWI. As per the MWI, each quantum occasion brings about the stretching of the universe into various equal universes, each comparing to an alternate result of the occasion. While the MWI stays a question of hypothetical discussion, it offers a novel point of view on the idea of quantum reality and the potential outcomes of different existing together aspects.

In the MWI, quantum occasions, for example, the twist of an electron or the rot of a radioactive molecule lead to the making of isolated parts of the real world, each addressing an alternate result. This translation challenges our traditional comprehension of quantum mechanics, in which particles are portrayed as existing in superpositions of states until noticed.

The ramifications of the MWI stretch out to the domain of quantum processing, where the idea of quantum superposition is tackled for computational purposes. Quantum PCs influence the capability of equal handling by performing computations in numerous states at the same time. This ability holds the commitment of reforming fields like cryptography, enhancement, and reproductions.

The idea of quantum registering in an equal reality brings up issues about the effect on encryption and information security. With the possibility to break conventional encryption techniques, quantum processing moves our capacity to safeguard delicate data in our current reality where equal real factors and quantum superposition are a reality.

7.3 The impact of "what if" questions on our understanding of reality

"Consider the possibility that" questions are amazing assets of human interest and creative mind, permitting us to investigate the tremendous spread of conceivable outcomes and think about how our reality could be different under different conditions. These requests urge us to challenge the limits of our ongoing comprehension of the real world, question our presumptions, and consider elective results that might have molded our reality. As we dig into the effect of "imagine a scenario in which" inquiries on how we might interpret reality, we reveal their significant impact on different features of human existence, from logical request and philosophical examination to writing, direction, and self-awareness.

At the core of "imagine a scenario in which" questions lies the investigation of expected elective results and the reevaluation of previous occasions or choices. These inquiries act as scholarly jungle gyms, where we take part in psychological studies to imagine real factors that vary from our own. They brief us to inspect the outcomes of various decisions and activities, empowering us to see the world through another focal point.

In the domain of logical request and trial and error, "consider the possibility that" questions are basic to speculation testing and examination plan. Researchers and analysts utilize these inquiries to investigate likely results and guide the advancement of tests. By taking into account a scope of "imagine a scenario in which" situations, they can distinguish basic factors and strategies that might yield important experiences. These situations are a foundation of different logical disciplines, from material science and science to brain research.

One conspicuous illustration of the utilization of "consider the possibility that" inquiries in logical request is the psychological test. Psychological tests are hypothetical situations made by researchers and scholars to inspect perplexing and theoretical ideas. These situations permit specialists to investigate the results of various premises and suppositions, assisting them with acquiring further experiences into the peculiarities they study.

For example, Albert Einstein's perception of riding close by a light emission prompted the improvement of his hypothesis of unique relativity. This psychological study tested the conventional comprehension of reality and changed our impression of the universe. Essentially, Erwin Schrödinger's fanciful feline in a fixed box outlined the Catch 22 of quantum superposition, bringing up issues about the idea of the real world and estimation in the quantum world.

In navigation and critical thinking, "imagine a scenario where" questions assume a crucial part in technique improvement and chance evaluation. These inquiries urge people and associations to think about a great many expected results and form alternate courses of action. By imagining different "consider the possibility that" situations, they can settle on informed choices, plan for possibilities, and explore complex difficulties successfully.

In finance, "consider the possibility that" situations are utilized for risk examination and speculation techniques. Examiners and portfolio directors utilize these situations to survey the possible effect of different monetary, market, and international improvements on ventures and monetary business sectors. These situations assist financial backers with planning for various results and pursue informed choices to relieve risk and boost returns.

One broadly perceived illustration of "consider the possibility that" situations in finance is pressure trying, where monetary organizations assess their flexibility under extreme financial circumstances. These tests help banks, insurance agency, and other monetary elements survey their capacity to endure financial shocks and emergencies. By taking into account a scope of unfriendly situations, they can guarantee their steadiness and monetary sufficiency.

In day to day existence, individuals use "imagine a scenario where" inquiries to explore many individual choices and difficulties. Whether they are thinking about vocation decisions, connections, or way of life changes, people frequently ask themselves inquiries like "Consider the possibility that I seek after this profession way?" or "Consider the possibility that I make this venture?" These situations assist people with weighing expected results, assess dangers, and imagine how their decisions could deeply mold their lives.

In the domain of writing, "consider the possibility that" situations are a focal component of sci-fi and speculative fiction. Creators in these types frequently suggest conversation starters like "Consider the possibility that people could go through time?" or "Consider the possibility that we experienced extraterrestrial life?" to make inventive stories that investigate the ramifications of such situations. These accounts welcome perusers to ponder the outcomes of logical headways, cultural changes, and humankind's communication with different creatures and universes.

H.G. Wells' book "The Conflict of the Universes" is an exemplary illustration of a "consider the possibility that" situation in writing. The story imagines a reality where Earth is attacked by mechanically progressed Martians, offering a reflection on human weakness and flexibility when faced with an exceptionally progressed outsider civilization. Additionally, Philip K. Dick's "The Man in the High Palace" investigates an other history situation wherein the Hub powers won The Second Great War, bringing up issues about the impact of authentic occasions and the delicacy of the real world.

In mainstream society, "consider the possibility that" situations are necessary to the idea of substitute real factors and equal universes. The possibility of various aspects or equal universes gives a material to narrating and inspecting the results of different decisions and occasions. Whether it is the idea of a mirror universe in the "Star Journey" establishment or the "multiverse" in superhuman comics, these situations offer a stage for imaginative narrating and investigating the effect of decisions on the real world.

For example, in the Wonder Artistic Universe, the idea of the multiverse has become key to the account. The film "Specialist Weird" presents fanning real factors and the significance of safeguarding the soundness of the multiverse. This idea makes way for future storylines in what characters explore substitute aspects and equal universes, bringing "consider the possibility that" situations to life on the big screen.

In philosophical talk, "imagine a scenario in which" situations act as vehicles for investigating psychological tests that test key inquiries regarding presence, ethical quality, and the idea of the real world. These situations brief savants to scrutinize their suppositions, challenge their convictions, and dig into the intricacies of moral difficulties.

The "streetcar issue" is an exemplary illustration of a "consider the possibility that" situation in way of thinking. This psychological test presents a situation in which an individual should choose whether to redirect an out of control streetcar that would somehow hurt various people. The situation features the strain between utilitarian morals, which focus on everyone's benefit, and deontological morals, which accentuate adherence to moral standards. By looking at such situations, savants intend to acquire a more profound comprehension of moral and moral independent direction.

In the area of innovation and designing, "consider the possibility that" situations are fundamental for development and hazard evaluation. Architects and originators utilize these situations to think about likely disappointments, weaknesses, and security measures while growing new items and frameworks. By inspecting different "consider the possibility that" situations, they can recognize shortcomings, expect issues, and devise arrangements that guarantee the unwavering quality and security of their manifestations.

In the field of advanced plane design, "consider the possibility that" situations are especially applicable. While planning space apparatus, engineers should represent a large number of speculative situations, including hardware glitches, gravitational powers, and the difficulties of reemergence into Earth's climate. These situations drive the advancement of frameworks and conventions to guarantee the security of space travelers and the progress of missions.

In medical services and clinical exploration, "consider the possibility that" situations are instrumental in analyzing the expected impacts of sicknesses, therapies, and mediations.

Disease transmission specialists and general wellbeing specialists have utilized situation examination to figure the spread of sicknesses, evaluate the effects of different control measures, and guide leaders in answering general wellbeing emergencies.

One of the most noticeable late instances of "consider the possibility that" situations in medical care is the utilization of models to estimate the spread of Coronavirus and evaluate the impacts of different regulation measures. Disease transmission specialists and general wellbeing specialists have utilized situation examination to expect medical services framework requests, assess the adequacy of immunization missions, and guide chiefs in answering the pandemic.

In the domain of global relations and strategy, "consider the possibility that" situations are vital to key preparation and compromise. Policymakers and negotiators consider different situations to expect international turns of events and survey possible results. By inspecting these situations, they can figure out international strategies, arrange arrangements, and explore complex worldwide relations successfully.

One persevering through illustration of "consider the possibility that" situations in worldwide relations is the Virus War and the idea of "commonly guaranteed annihilation" (Frantic). During the Virus War, both the US and the Soviet Association had enormous stockpiles of atomic weapons. The "consider the possibility that" situation of an atomic clash highlighted the overwhelming outcomes that would result from such a contention, at last filling in as an impediment against the utilization of atomic weapons.

In schooling, "consider the possibility that" situations offer important devices for improving decisive reasoning and critical thinking abilities. Instructors utilize theoretical situations to draw in understudies, advance imaginative reasoning, and urge them to think about a scope of potential results. These situations encourage scholarly interest and assist understudies with fostering the ability to assess decisions and results.

Chapter 8

Realities Beyond Our Own

The human creative mind has forever been charmed by the possibility of real factors past our own, domains that exist outside the extent of our ordinary experience and understanding. This interest with the obscure and the unfamiliar regions of presence has led to an abundance of speculative idea, philosophical request, and inventive narrating. In the journey to investigate real factors past our own, we make the ways for the creative mind, think about the conceivable outcomes of equal universes, think about the idea of extraterrestrial life, and dig into the profundities of the human brain.

Quite possibly of the most interesting idea that lead us to consider real factors past our own is equal universes, frequently connected with the multiverse speculation. This theory recommends that there might be different universes or aspects coinciding close by our own, each with its own arrangement of actual regulations, occasions, and conceivable outcomes. In these equal universes, the circumstances for presence and the course of history might be unfathomably not the same as what we know in our world.

The idea of equal universes challenges our traditional comprehension of a particular and direct reality, where situation unfurl in a foreordained succession. All things considered, it recommends that each decision, activity, or occasion might prompt a fanning of real factors, making a huge and interconnected multiverse of potential outcomes. This idea urges us to pose inquiries, for example, "Consider the possibility that authentic situation had transpired in an unexpected way?" or "Imagine a scenario where actual constants had different qualities?" In investigating these "imagine a scenario where" situations, we ponder how the world may be different in these substitute aspects.

In the domain of hypothetical material science and cosmology, the idea of the multiverse has acquired unmistakable quality. The Many-Universes Translation (MWI) of quantum mechanics, for instance, recommends that each quantum occasion brings about the spreading of the universe into numerous equal universes, each relating to an alternate result of the occasion. While the MWI stays an issue of hypothetical discussion, it offers an interesting point of view on the idea of quantum reality and the conceivable outcomes of numerous existing together aspects.

The possibility of limitless variety inside the multiverse is a convincing part of considering real factors past our own. In a multiverse, each possible variety of reality might exist, from unpretentious contrasts in our regular routines to significant shifts in the direction of history and the laws of physical science themselves.

This welcomes us to envision universes where the Roman Realm never fell, where the Modern Upheaval happened in old China, or where gravity and the speed of light have various qualities.

For instance, in an equal reality where the Roman Domain never fell, the Western world could have encountered a continuous tradition of Roman administration, culture, and impact. The improvement of science, innovation, and craftsmanship might have followed a particular direction, influencing the worldwide overall influence and the state of world developments.

Likewise, in reality as we know it where the Modern Upset happened in old China, the course of mechanical progression and worldwide exchange could have followed something else entirely. China might have arisen as a modern superpower, altogether affecting the cutting edge world. The results of such a situation reach out to financial frameworks, international elements, and social trades.

Equal universes additionally reaches out to the domain of individual decisions and the idea of the "butterfly impact." This guideline recommends that little introductory changes can prompt huge downstream results. In equal universes, these minor changes in choices and activities can swell outward to make altogether various results.

Envision an existence where verifiable figures settled on various decisions. For example, "Consider the possibility that Abraham Lincoln had not sought after a political vocation?" Such a situation could prompt a substitute reality in which the American Nationwide conflict unfurled in an unexpected way, modifying the destiny of the US and the worldwide scene. The exchange between individual organization and verifiable occasions is a charming part of considering real factors past our own.

Besides, the laws of physical science themselves might change in these equal real factors. The constants and principal powers that administer our universe could take on various qualities, prompting assorted actual real factors. Guessing about such varieties prompts questions like, "Consider the possibility that gravity were more vulnerable?" or "Imagine a scenario in which the speed of light were unique."

In our current reality where gravity is more vulnerable, the consequences for divine bodies, the construction of systems, and the development of life could be emphatically particular. The actual texture of the real world, insofar as we can tell, would be modified. Essentially, changes in the speed of light could reshape the idea of causality, time, and the conceivable outcomes of interstellar travel.

The idea of equal real factors additionally stretches out to inquiries regarding the presence of extraterrestrial life. In a huge multiverse, it becomes conceivable to contrastingly imagine universes where clever life has developed.

The circumstances forever, the structures it takes, and the potential for interstellar correspondence might fluctuate generally in these equal real factors.

In one equal reality, life might have emerged on a planet with fundamentally unique natural circumstances, bringing about creatures with exceptional variations and capacities. In another, shrewd civilizations could have created elective methods of correspondence and travel, connecting with them a mind boggling and charming undertaking.

One of the getting through questions related with equal truths is the idea of the "reflect universe." Promoted in sci-fi, the mirror universe is an other reality that fills in as a dull or wound impression of our own. In this situation, natural characters and elements exist in an equal reality with differentiating virtues, inspirations, and results.

The idea of the mirror universe brings up provocative issues about human instinct, ethical quality, and the job of decision in molding our predeterminations. It prompts us to investigate how different moral and social systems could prompt fundamentally unique cultural standards and ways of behaving. This investigation can act as a mirror to our own reality, empowering us to reconsider our qualities and think about the effect of our decisions.

In writing and mainstream society, the idea of the multiverse and equal real factors has led to endless imaginative stories. Sci-fi creators and movie producers frequently utilize these thoughts as a material for narrating and investigation. They create substitute universes and situations to look at the results of various decisions, mechanical headways, and cultural designs.

A perfect representation of this is the "Star Trip" establishment, which presented the idea of a mirror universe in a few of its series. In this equal reality, recognizable characters take on changed jobs and moral arrangements. This story gadget offers watchers a charming point of view because of decisions and moral choices on the course of history and individual predeterminations.

Likewise, the "Many-Universes Translation" of quantum mechanics proposes that each conceivable result of a quantum occasion exists in a different part of the multiverse. This understanding has motivated interesting works of fiction that investigate the ramifications of this thought. The film "Sliding Entryways" presents two equal real factors in light of a basic second in time, demonstrating the way that little choices can prompt tremendously unique life directions.

The idea of equal truths isn't bound to the domain of fiction and speculative idea. It additionally tracks down reverberation in the field of quantum material science, where it is related with the MWI. As per the MWI, each quantum occasion brings about the fanning of the universe into numerous equal universes, each comparing to an alternate result of the occasion.

While the MWI stays a question of hypothetical discussion, it offers a special point of view on the idea of quantum reality and the conceivable outcomes of different coinciding aspects.

In the MWI, quantum occasions, for example, the twist of an electron or the rot of a radioactive particle lead to the production of isolated parts of the real world, each addressing an alternate result. This translation challenges our customary comprehension of quantum mechanics, in which particles are depicted as existing in superpositions of states until noticed.

The ramifications of the MWI stretch out to the domain of quantum registering, where the idea of quantum superposition is saddled for computational purposes. Quantum PCs influence the capability of equal handling by performing computations in various states all the while. This capacity holds the commitment of reforming fields like cryptography, enhancement, and reproductions.

The idea of quantum figuring in an equal reality brings up issues about the effect on encryption and information security. With the possibility to break customary encryption techniques, quantum processing provokes our capacity to safeguard delicate data in reality as we know it where equal real factors and quantum superposition are a reality. This situation prompts specialists and specialists to foster new encryption strategies and safety efforts to shield information and correspondences.

Equal real factors additionally brief us to consider the limits of human comprehension and the constraints of our insight. The idea that we may just see a small portion of the multiverse brings up issues about the idea of the real world and our capacity to get a handle on its full extension. It urges us to consider the boundlessness of strange aspects that might lie past our tactile encounters.

8.1 Scientific exploration of potential parallel worlds

The idea of equal universes or equal universes has for some time been an enthralling subject of logical investigation, philosophical request, and inventive hypothesis. It challenges how we might interpret reality and prompts us to consider the presence of coinciding aspects that might contrast from our own in essential ways. While equal universes has customarily been related with sci-fi and speculative idea, it has likewise earned respect and consideration inside the domain of logical examination. This investigation looks to overcome any issues among hypothesis and experimental proof, planning to test and approve the presence of equal universes through different logical methodologies.

At the center of the idea of equal universes lies that numerous universes or aspects might exist close by our own, each with its own arrangement of actual regulations, occasions, and conceivable outcomes. This thought is frequently connected with the multiverse speculation, which proposes that the universe we see is only one of numerous in an immense multiverse.

These equal universes might exist together autonomously, each with its interesting circumstances and results.

The idea of equal universes challenges the conventional direct model of the real world, where situation unfurl in a foreordained grouping. All things being equal, it suggests that each decision, activity, or occasion could prompt an expanding of real factors, making an immense and interconnected snare of potential outcomes. These conceivable outcomes urge us to pose inquiries, for example, "Imagine a scenario in which verifiable situation had transpired in an unexpected way?" or "Consider the possibility that the laws of material science were on a very basic level modified?" In this investigation, we dive into the logical methodologies and hypothetical structures that have been created to look at the expected presence of equal universes.

One of the hypothetical systems that has acquired conspicuousness in the logical investigation of equal universes is the Many-Universes Understanding (MWI) of quantum mechanics. Proposed by physicist Hugh Everett III in 1957, the MWI recommends that each quantum occasion brings about the spreading of the universe into numerous equal universes, each relating to an alternate result of the occasion. As per the MWI, quantum superposition permits particles to exist in different states at the same time until they are estimated or noticed. This translation challenges the customary Copenhagen understanding, where particles exist in a solitary state until noticed.

In the MWI, quantum occasions, for example, the twist of an electron or the rot of a radioactive molecule lead to the production of isolated parts of the real world, each addressing an alternate result. While the MWI stays an issue of hypothetical discussion, it offers a special viewpoint on the idea of quantum reality and the potential outcomes of various existing together aspects.

One of the critical elements of the MWI is the possibility that each conceivable quantum result really happens in a different part of the multiverse. For example, on the off chance that an electron can turn up or down, as per the MWI, the two results happen in discrete parts of the multiverse. This translation challenges our ordinary comprehension of quantum mechanics, where particles are depicted as existing in superpositions of states until noticed.

The MWI has significant ramifications for the idea of the real world and our place inside it. It recommends that each decision, each quantum occasion, and each estimation prompts the production of equal universes, each with its exceptional arrangement of results. This viewpoint has been both lauded for its tastefulness and censured for its calculated intricacy.

To show the ramifications of the MWI, consider the popular Schrödinger's feline psychological test. In this situation, a feline is put in a fixed box with a radioactive iota that has a half possibility rotting and delivering poison, which would kill the feline. As per the MWI, until the case is opened and the feline is noticed, it exists in a superposition of states.

In one part of the multiverse, the feline is alive, while in another branch, the feline is dead. This analysis effectively features the bizarre and outlandish nature of quantum reality as depicted by the MWI.

With regards to logical investigation, the MWI has incited analysts to consider the ramifications of quantum fanning and the potential for observational tests. While direct trial check of the MWI stays testing, there have been endeavors to foster analyses and perceptions that could give backhanded proof to the presence of equal universes.

One such methodology is the investigation of quantum entrapment, a peculiarity wherein particles become corresponded so that the condition of one molecule is reliant upon the condition of another, in any event, when they are isolated by enormous distances. Trap difficulties our traditional comprehension of causality and region, proposing that data can be traded between particles quickly, apparently rising above the speed of light.

Tests in quantum snare have prompted the suggestion that the peculiarity may be made sense of by the presence of equal universes. As per this understanding, snared particles in our universe are associated with their partners in other equal universes, where they share data. This viewpoint offers a potential clarification for the apparently non-nearby way of behaving of entrapped particles.

Specialists have led investigations to test the snare speculation, and keeping in mind that results have not conclusively affirmed the presence of equal universes, they have given charming bits of knowledge into the idea of quantum trap. The field of quantum mechanics keeps on pushing the limits of how we might interpret the quantum world, offering new roads for investigating the idea of equal universes.

One more road of logical investigation of equal universes is the investigation of the grandiose microwave foundation radiation (CMB), the phosphorescence of the Enormous detonation. The CMB is a weak sparkle of radiation that penetrates the universe and gives basic experiences into the early history of the universe. Researchers have inspected the CMB for abnormalities or examples that could propose the impact of equal universes.

One speculation is that the CMB could convey engraves from crashes or cooperations between our universe and equal universes. Such associations might have left perceivable marks in the CMB, which, whenever noticed, would give aberrant proof of equal universes. While research in this space is continuous, no authoritative proof has arisen to help this theory.

In cosmology, the idea of the multiverse has additionally been investigated through the investigation of astronomical expansion. Grandiose expansion is a hypothesis that proposes the universe went through a fast and remarkable extension not long after the Huge explosion.

This hypothesis has been upheld by different galactic perceptions, yet it has additionally prompted the possibility of an "inflationary multiverse."

As indicated by the inflationary multiverse speculation, various locales of the universe might have gone through changing paces of expansion, prompting the development of air pocket like spaces with particular actual properties. Every one of these air pocket spaces could address a different universe with its own arrangement of actual regulations. The inflationary multiverse speculation offers a potential component for the age of equal universes inside a more extensive multiverse structure.

While the inflationary multiverse speculation stays speculative and is dependent upon progressing examination and discussion, it features the interconnectedness of cosmology and the investigation of equal universes. It urges us to consider the beginnings and properties of the universe with regards to a multiverse that reaches out past our own existence.

The investigation of equal universes has additionally found reverberation in the field of quantum registering. Quantum registering use the standards of quantum mechanics, including the idea of superposition, to perform computations and recreations that are infeasible for traditional PCs. Quantum PCs can possibly change different fields, from cryptography and improvement to materials science and medication revelation.

With regards to quantum figuring, the presence of equal universes turns into a fundamental rule. Quantum bits or qubits can exist in superpositions of states, permitting quantum PCs to at the same time perform estimations in different states. This ability holds the commitment of tackling complex issues and reproductions more effectively than old style PCs.

One of the most notable quantum calculations that exhibits the force of equal handling is Shor's calculation. Shor's calculation is intended to consider enormous numbers their superb parts, an errand that is profoundly trying for old style PCs. The calculation use quantum parallelism to investigate numerous conceivable outcomes at the same time, making it altogether quicker than traditional calculations for factorization.

The capability of quantum registering in equal universes thely affects encryption and information security. With the capacity to break conventional encryption techniques, quantum registering provokes our capacity to safeguard delicate data in this present reality where equal real factors and quantum superposition are a reality. This situation prompts specialists and specialists to foster new encryption methods and safety efforts to protect information and correspondences in a quantum world.

One way to deal with tending to the security challenges presented by quantum registering is the advancement of post-quantum cryptography. Post-quantum cryptography centers around planning encryption strategies that are impervious to quantum assaults.

Specialists are investigating different cryptographic procedures, for example, cross section based cryptography, code-based cryptography, and multivariate polynomial cryptography, to give secure options in a quantum world.

The capability of equal universes with regards to quantum registering offers an intriguing combination of hypothetical material science and reasonable applications. It highlights the significant effect that the investigation of equal universes can have on arising advances and the fate of registering.

Equal real factors additionally brief us to consider the limits of human comprehension and the limits of our discernment. The idea that we may just see a small portion of the multiverse brings up issues about the idea of the real world and our capacity to get a handle on its full degree. It urges us to consider the boundlessness of unfamiliar aspects that might lie past our tactile encounters.

In the area of brain research, the idea of equal real factors associates with the investigation of changed conditions of awareness. A few people report encounters in which they see substitute aspects, experience creatures from equal real factors, or excursion into new scenes of the brain. These records challenge how we might interpret the idea of awareness and the connection between abstract encounters and objective reality.

The investigation of modified conditions of cognizance has been a subject of revenue in brain science, neuroscience, and the investigation of human discernment. Changed states can be initiated through different techniques, like contemplation, hallucinogenic substances, and tactile hardship. These states frequently include a change in the singular's impression of the real world, prompting significant encounters and bits of knowledge.

For instance, people who take part in profound contemplation might report encounters of greatness or solidarity with the universe. These encounters propose that changed conditions of cognizance can make the way for various methods of insight and mindfulness. While these modified states don't be guaranteed to give direct proof of equal universes, they feature the pliability of human cognizance and investigating various aspects of reality potential.

In the domain of shamanic rehearses and customary native conviction frameworks, the investigation of modified conditions of cognizance is a focal component of social and profound practices. Shamans and specialists frequently depict encounters in which they enter equal real factors to acquire experiences, get recuperating, or speak with soul substances.

Shamanic ventures include the utilization of customs, music, and now and again psychoactive substances to prompt adjusted conditions of awareness. During these excursions, people might report experiences with creatures from equal real factors, like creature spirits, predecessors, or heavenly elements.

These encounters hold profound social and otherworldly importance and are viewed as a method for getting to information and recuperating from the inconspicuous domains.

The investigation of shamanic rehearses and the encounters of people who enter changed conditions of cognizance has suggestions for how we might interpret human discernment and the limits of the real world. While these encounters may not give exact proof to resemble universes, they welcome us to examine the secrets of cognizance and the manners by which our abstract encounters can rise above the impediments of normal insight.

The idea of equal real factors additionally tracks down reverberation in different social and profound customs all over the planet. Native conviction frameworks frequently integrate interconnected aspects and equal universes occupied by spirits, precursors, and heavenly creatures. These convictions advance comprehension we might interpret assorted cosmologies and the manners by which various societies see the texture of the real world.

For instance, in numerous native societies, there is a faith in the presence of a soul world or a hereditary domain that exists lined up with the actual world. These equal aspects are occupied by spirits, predecessors, and other heavenly elements. Native practices frequently include customs, functions, and correspondence with these powerful creatures to look for direction, mending, and insurance.

The idea of equal universes in native conviction frameworks fills in as a demonstration of the variety of human social and profound articulations. It helps us to remember the rich woven artwork of perspectives that exist across various social orders and the meaning of these convictions in shaping the lives and personalities of people and networks.

All in all, the logical investigation of potential equal universes is a complicated and multi-layered try that crosses the limits of physical science, cosmology, quantum mechanics, and arising advancements. While the idea of equal universes has been a subject of interest and discussion, it keeps on rousing specialists to foster hypothetical systems and trial moves toward that might reveal insight into its presence.

The Many-Universes Translation of quantum mechanics challenges how we might interpret quantum reality and the potential for fanning equal universes with each quantum occasion. While the MWI stays a subject of hypothetical discussion, it has incited researchers to look at peculiarities, for example, quantum entrapment and the enormous microwave foundation radiation for proof of equal universes.

The inflationary multiverse speculation in cosmology proposes that bubble-like areas with unmistakable actual properties might have shaped during astronomical expansion, prompting the formation of equal universes. This idea highlights the interconnectedness of cosmology and the investigation of equal universes.

8.2 Current research and theories in quantum mechanics

Quantum mechanics, the principal hypothesis that oversees the way of behaving of particles at the littlest scales, has been a wellspring of interest, interest, and significant logical revelation since its commencement in the mid twentieth hundred years. It has prompted pivotal advances in innovation and our comprehension of the universe. Throughout the long term, quantum mechanics has proceeded to advance and grow, leading to new research bearings, hypotheses, and investigations that challenge our past originations of the real world. In this investigation, we will dig into momentum examination and hypotheses in quantum mechanics, revealing insight into the boondocks of this charming field.

1. **Quantum Snare and Chime's Hypothesis**
   Quantum snare stays one of the most confounding and fascinating parts of quantum mechanics. It alludes to a peculiarity where particles become connected so that the condition of one molecule is reliant upon the condition of another, in any event, when they are isolated by huge distances. This non-nearby association between trapped particles has intrigued researchers and prompted weighty trials.

   Chime's Hypothesis, planned by physicist John Ringer during the 1960s, gave a method for testing the idea of quantum snare. Chime's Disparity, got from his hypothesis, depicts specific measurable relationships that should turn out as expected for any hypothesis that complies with the standards of territory and authenticity. In any case, quantum mechanics predicts an infringement of Chime's Imbalance, demonstrating that the world is non-nearby and doesn't stick to old style authenticity.

   Ongoing investigations, for example, those including ensnared photons and infringement of Chime imbalances, have major areas of strength for given to the legitimacy of quantum trap and the infringement of old style authenticity. These examinations keep on being refined and expanded, investigating the restrictions of trap and testing the underpinnings of quantum hypothesis.

2. **Quantum Data and Quantum Processing**
   Quantum data science is a quickly developing field that investigates the remarkable properties of quantum frameworks to foster novel strategies for data handling and correspondence. Quantum PCs, specifically, stand out enough to be noticed because of their capability to perform complex computations dramatically quicker than old style PCs.

   One of the critical ideas in quantum registering is the qubit, the quantum simple of an old style bit. Qubits can exist in superpositions of states, permitting quantum PCs to at the same time investigate different conceivable outcomes. Calculations, for example, Shor's calculation and Grover's calculation have shown the potential for quantum PCs to take care of issues in cryptography, improvement, and information search substantially more effectively than old style PCs.

   Late exploration in quantum registering centers around building down to earth quantum gadgets, creating blunder amendment codes, and tending to difficulties in increasing quantum processors. Organizations and examination establishments are effectively chipping away at quantum equipment and programming to saddle the force of quantum calculation.

3. **Quantum Correspondence and Cryptography**
   Quantum mechanics likewise offers a progressive way to deal with secure

correspondence through quantum key dispersion (QKD) and quantum cryptography. QKD depends on the standards of quantum snare to empower secure and solid correspondence channels.

In QKD, two gatherings share ensnared qubits and use them to make a common mystery key. Any endeavor to snoop on the correspondence can be distinguished since estimating a trapped qubit unavoidably alters its state. Ongoing progressions in quantum correspondence have prompted the improvement of quantum organizations and the fruitful show of significant distance quantum key conveyance.

Research in quantum cryptography keeps on tending to pragmatic difficulties, for example, creating quantum repeaters for expanding the scope of secure correspondence and streamlining quantum conventions for certifiable applications.

4. **Quantum Test systems and Quantum AI**

Quantum test systems are specific quantum gadgets intended to recreate complex quantum frameworks that are challenging to review with traditional PCs. They can possibly investigate quantum peculiarities, test essential speculations, and reproduce quantum materials and particles.

Quantum AI is an arising field that use quantum PCs and test systems to improve AI calculations. Quantum calculations can speed up errands like streamlining, design acknowledgment, and information examination. Late examination in this space centers around the advancement of quantum calculations for commonsense AI applications, and the joining of quantum figuring with old style AI systems.

5. **Quantum Sensors and Metrology**

Quantum sensors, like nuclear clocks and quantum magnetometers, use the accuracy of quantum frameworks to quantify actual amounts with extraordinary exactness. Nuclear clocks, for instance, depend on the superposition of energy states in particles to keep time with striking accuracy. They are essential to worldwide situating frameworks (GPS), broadcast communications, and logical examination.

Quantum-improved sensors have applications in different fields, including geophysics, route, clinical imaging, and central physical science. Continuous examination intends to push the limits of responsiveness and foster new quantum sensors for a great many applications.

6. **Quantum Establishments and Understandings**

The understanding of quantum mechanics stays a subject of philosophical and logical discussion. Different translations, like the Copenhagen understanding, Many-Universes Understanding (MWI), and the pilot-wave hypothesis, offer various approaches to grasping the idea of quantum reality.

The Many-Universes Understanding, specifically, keeps on being a subject of interest and discussion. It recommends that each quantum occasion brings about the stretching of the universe into various equal universes, each comparing to an alternate result of the occasion. While the MWI stays an issue of hypothetical discussion, continuous exploration investigates its suggestions for quantum cosmology and the underpinnings of quantum hypothesis.

7. **Quantum Metrology and Accuracy Estimations**

Quantum metrology use the standards of quantum mechanics to accomplish estimations with phenomenal accuracy. It includes procedures, for example, quantum-upgraded interferometry, where the quantum properties of particles empower the estimation of actual amounts with unprecedented precision.

This examination has applications in many fields, including basic material science, geodesy, and gravitational wave location. The advancement of quantum sensors and metrology methods is a functioning area of examination, with the possibility to upset our capacity to gauge and grasp the actual world.

8. **Quantum Materials and Quantum Advances**

Quantum materials are substances with exceptional electronic and attractive properties that arise at the quantum level. Research in quantum materials investigates their expected applications in quantum advancements, for example, quantum sensors, quantum figuring, and quantum correspondence.

Materials with topological properties, like topological separators and superconductors, are exceptionally compelling. They can possibly uphold the formation of strong and mistake safe quantum gadgets. Late examination in quantum materials centers around orchestrating new materials and grasping their quantum properties.

9. **Quantum Thermodynamics**

Quantum thermodynamics is an interdisciplinary field that joins standards of quantum mechanics with the laws of thermodynamics. It looks to figure out the thermodynamic way of behaving of quantum frameworks at the infinitesimal level, where quantum impacts become critical.

Research in quantum thermodynamics investigates the productivity of quantum motors, the thermodynamics of quantum data handling, and the job of quantum lucidness in energy trade. This field has suggestions for the advancement of more effective energy transformation and data handling innovations.

10. **Quantum Science**

Quantum mechanics is progressively being applied to the investigation of natural frameworks. Quantum science explores the job of quantum peculiarities in organic cycles, like photosynthesis, catalyst responses, and the working of natural atoms.

Research in quantum science tries to reveal how quantum soundness and ensnarement add to the productivity and power of natural frameworks. It can possibly propel how we might interpret life at the sub-atomic level and move new ways to deal with bioengineering and medication.

8.3 The quest to discover evidence of alternate realities

The journey to find proof of substitute real factors, equal universes, or different aspects has long caught the human creative mind and the interest of researchers and scientists. This interest with the presence of different domains past our own has driven investigations in different fields, from hypothetical material science and cosmology to reasoning and mysticism. While the idea of substitute real factors has frequently been related with sci-fi and speculative idea, contemporary science has left on an excursion to look for observational proof that could affirm or invalidate the presence of equal universes.

Quite possibly of the most fascinating idea in the investigation of substitute truths is the possibility of the multiverse, which proposes that there might be numerous universes or aspects existing together close by our own. Every one of these universes might have its special arrangement of actual regulations, occasions, and conceivable outcomes, which could contrast altogether from what we see in our existence. The multiverse speculation challenges our traditional comprehension of a solitary and straight reality, proposing that each decision, activity, or occasion might prompt a stretching of real factors, making an immense and interconnected multiverse of potential outcomes.

The idea of equal universes has been vital to the multiverse speculation, which has acquired unmistakable quality in the domain of hypothetical physical science and cosmology. The Many-Universes Translation (MWI) of quantum mechanics, proposed by Hugh Everett III in 1957, recommends that each quantum occasion brings about the stretching of the universe into various equal universes, each relating to an alternate result of the occasion.

The MWI challenges our customary translation of quantum mechanics, where particles exist in superpositions of states until noticed. In the MWI, quantum occasions, like the twist of an electron or the rot of a radioactive iota, lead to the making of discrete parts of the real world, each addressing an alternate result. This translation has significant ramifications for the idea of quantum reality and the potential outcomes of numerous existing together aspects.

The possibility of boundless variety inside the multiverse is a charming part of thinking about substitute real factors. In a multiverse, each possible variety of reality might exist, from unpretentious contrasts in our day to day routines to significant shifts in the direction of history and the laws of physical science themselves.

This welcomes us to envision universes where the Roman Domain never fell, where the Modern Transformation happened in antiquated China, or where gravity and the speed of light have various qualities.

For example, in an equal reality where the Roman Domain never fell, the Western world could have encountered a continuous tradition of Roman administration, culture, and impact. The improvement of science, innovation, and workmanship might have followed a particular direction, influencing the worldwide overall influence and the state of world civilizations.

Likewise, in this present reality where the Modern Upset happened in old China, the course of mechanical progression and worldwide exchange could have followed something else altogether. China might have arisen as a modern superpower, altogether impacting the cutting edge world. The results of such a situation reach out to monetary frameworks, international elements, and social trades.

Equal universes additionally reaches out to the domain of individual decisions and the idea of the "butterfly impact." This guideline recommends that little beginning changes can prompt critical downstream results. In equal universes, these minor changes in choices and activities can swell outward to make completely various results.

Envision an existence where verifiable figures settled on various decisions. For example, "Consider the possibility that Abraham Lincoln had not sought after a political profession?" Such a situation could prompt a substitute reality in which the American Nationwide conflict unfurled in an unexpected way, modifying the destiny of the US and the worldwide scene. The interaction between individual organization and verifiable occasions is a charming part of thinking about substitute real factors.

Moreover, the laws of material science themselves might shift in these equal real factors. The constants and basic powers that oversee our universe could take on various qualities, prompting assorted actual real factors. Estimating about such varieties prompts questions like, "Imagine a scenario where gravity were more fragile?" or "Consider the possibility that the speed of light were unique."

In this present reality where gravity is more fragile, the consequences for divine bodies, the design of cosmic systems, and the development of life could be emphatically particular. The actual texture of the real world, as far as we can tell, would be changed. Likewise, changes in the speed of light could reshape the idea of causality, time, and the conceivable outcomes of interstellar travel.

The idea of substitute real factors additionally stretches out to inquiries regarding the presence of extraterrestrial life. In a huge multiverse, it becomes conceivable to contrastingly imagine universes where savvy life has developed.

The circumstances forever, the structures it takes, and the potential for interstellar correspondence might fluctuate broadly in these equal real factors.

In one equal reality, life might have emerged on a planet with profoundly unique ecological circumstances, bringing about organic entities with remarkable variations and capacities. In another, shrewd civilizations could have created elective methods of correspondence and travel, connecting with them a mind boggling and fascinating undertaking.

One of the getting through questions related with substitute truths is the idea of the "reflect universe." Promoted in sci-fi, the mirror universe is an other reality that fills in as a dim or turned impression of our own. In this situation, natural characters and elements exist in an equal reality with differentiating virtues, inspirations, and results.

The idea of the mirror universe brings up provocative issues about human instinct, ethical quality, and the job of decision in forming our fates. It prompts us to investigate how different moral and social systems could prompt fundamentally unique cultural standards and ways of behaving. This investigation can act as a mirror to our own reality, empowering us to reexamine our qualities and think about the effect of our decisions.

In writing and mainstream society, the idea of the multiverse and substitute real factors has led to endless imaginative stories. Sci-fi creators and movie producers frequently utilize these thoughts as a material for narrating and investigation. They create substitute universes and situations to look at the results of various decisions, innovative headways, and cultural designs.

A great representation of this is the "Star Trip" establishment, which presented the idea of a mirror universe in a few of its series. In this equal reality, natural characters take on changed jobs and moral arrangements. This story gadget offers watchers an enthralling point of view because of decisions and moral choices on the course of history and individual predeterminations.

Likewise, the "Many-Universes Translation" of quantum mechanics proposes that each conceivable result of a quantum occasion exists in a different part of the multiverse. This understanding has motivated provocative works of fiction that investigate the ramifications of this thought. The film "Sliding Entryways" presents two equal real factors in view of a straightforward second in time, demonstrating the way that little choices can prompt immeasurably unique life directions.

The idea of substitute truths isn't bound to the domain of fiction and speculative idea. It additionally tracks down reverberation in the field of quantum physical science, where it is related with the MWI.

As per the MWI, each quantum occasion brings about the fanning of the universe into various equal universes, each comparing to an alternate result of the occasion. While the MWI stays an issue of hypothetical discussion, it offers a remarkable point of view on the idea of quantum reality and the potential outcomes of different existing together aspects.

In the MWI, quantum occasions, for example, the twist of an electron or the rot of a radioactive particle lead to the making of isolated parts of the real world, each addressing an alternate result. This translation challenges our customary comprehension of quantum mechanics, in which particles are depicted as existing in superpositions of states until noticed.

The ramifications of the MWI reach out to the domain of quantum processing, where the idea of quantum superposition is saddled for computational purposes. Quantum PCs influence the capability of equal handling by performing estimations in numerous states at the same time. This ability holds the commitment of reforming fields like cryptography, streamlining, and reenactments.

The idea of quantum registering in an equal reality brings up issues about the effect on encryption and information security. With the possibility to break conventional encryption techniques, quantum processing provokes our capacity to safeguard delicate data in this present reality where equal real factors and quantum superposition are a reality. This situation prompts analysts and specialists to foster new encryption strategies and safety efforts to shield information and interchanges.

Equal real factors likewise brief us to consider the limits of human comprehension and the impediments of our discernment. The thought that we may just see a small part of the multiverse brings up issues about the idea of the real world and our capacity to get a handle on its full extension. It urges us to consider the immeasurability of strange aspects that might lie past our tactile encounters.

In the area of brain science, the idea of equal real factors associates with the investigation of adjusted conditions of awareness. A few people report encounters in which they see substitute aspects, experience creatures from equal real factors, or excursion.

Chapter 9

Conclusion

The investigation of substitute real factors through the idea of equal universes is a diverse and profoundly convincing undertaking that has dazzled human creative mind and propelled logical request, philosophical reflection, and imaginative narrating. This investigation has taken us on an excursion that traverses the limits of material science, quantum mechanics, cosmology, and the profundities of human cognizance. As we close this investigation, we consider the significant inquiries, suggestions, and potential outcomes that emerge from equal universes.

All through our excursion, we have dug into the idea of the multiverse, a speculative structure that recommends the presence of various universes or aspects existing together close by our own. Inside the multiverse, every universe might have its remarkable arrangement of actual regulations, occasions, and potential outcomes, making a huge and interconnected trap of real factors. This idea challenges the ordinary thought of a solitary, direct reality and welcomes us to mull over the endless variety and intricacy of presence.

One of the focal hypothetical structures in the investigation of equal universes is the Many-Universes Translation (MWI) of quantum mechanics. Proposed by Hugh Everett III in 1957, the MWI sets that each quantum occasion brings about the spreading of the universe into various equal universes, each addressing an alternate result of the occasion. In the MWI, particles exist in superpositions of states until noticed, and each conceivable result of a quantum occasion happens in a different part of the multiverse.

The MWI has significant ramifications for how we might interpret the idea of quantum reality and the job of perception in molding the course of occasions. It challenges the customary Copenhagen understanding of quantum mechanics, where particles exist in a solitary state until noticed. While the MWI stays a subject of discussion and investigation, it offers a one of a kind viewpoint on the interconnectedness of quantum occasions and the making of equal real factors.

One of the vital highlights of the MWI is the possibility that each decision, each quantum occasion, and each estimation prompts the age of equal universes, each with its novel arrangement of results. This thought prompts us to consider the meaning of our decisions and activities in reality as we know it where each choice prompts a fanning of real factors. It urges us to consider the significant ramifications of individual organization and the interconnectedness of our decisions with the texture of the multiverse.

With regards to logical investigation, the MWI has motivated scientists to think about observational tests for the presence of equal universes. While direct exploratory confirmation of the MWI stays an imposing test, researchers have investigated peculiarities, for example, quantum ensnarement and infinite microwave foundation radiation for roundabout proof of equal universes.

Quantum ensnarement, a peculiarity in which particles become corresponded so that the condition of one molecule is subject to the condition of another, has prompted the recommendation that snared particles in our universe are associated with their partners in other equal universes. This translation offers a possible clarification for the apparently non-neighborhood conduct of snared particles. Trial of snare and the infringement of Ringer imbalances have given captivating experiences into the idea of quantum reality and the expected presence of equal universes.

The investigation of inestimable microwave foundation radiation (CMB), the glimmer of the Huge explosion, has additionally been a road for investigating proof of equal universes. Speculations propose that the CMB could convey engraves from collaborations or crashes between our universe and equal universes, leaving recognizable marks in the radiation. While research in this space is continuous, no authoritative proof has arisen to help this theory.

In cosmology, the idea of the multiverse is entwined with the hypothesis of astronomical expansion. Infinite expansion suggests that the universe went through a fast and remarkable development soon after the Enormous detonation. This hypothesis, upheld by different cosmic perceptions, has led to the thought of an "inflationary multiverse."

As indicated by the inflationary multiverse speculation, various districts of the universe might have encountered shifting paces of expansion, prompting the arrangement of air pocket like areas with unmistakable actual properties. Every one of these air pocket spaces could address a different universe with its own arrangement of actual regulations and occasions. The inflationary multiverse gives a system to the age of equal universes inside a more extensive multiverse structure.

While the inflationary multiverse speculation stays speculative and is dependent upon continuous examination and discussion, it highlights the interconnectedness of cosmology and the investigation of equal universes. It prompts us to consider the starting points and properties of the universe inside the setting of a multiverse that reaches out past our own existence.

The investigation of equal universes has reached out to the field of quantum processing, where the idea of quantum superposition is utilized for computational purposes. Quantum PCs utilize qubits that can exist in superpositions of states, empowering them to all the while perform computations in different states.

The capability of quantum figuring in equal universes brings up issues about its effect on encryption and information security. Quantum PCs can possibly break conventional encryption strategies, moving our capacity to safeguard delicate data in reality as we know it where equal real factors and quantum superposition are a reality. Specialists are effectively growing new encryption procedures and safety efforts to protect information and correspondences in a quantum world.

In lined up with the logical investigation of equal universes, the idea has additionally tracked down reverberation in the domain of human cognizance and adjusted conditions of mindfulness. Adjusted states, prompted through practices like contemplation, hallucinogenic substances, and tactile hardship, offer people the chance to see substitute aspects, experience creatures from equal real factors, and excursion into the unknown scenes of the brain.

The investigation of modified conditions of cognizance has been a subject of revenue in brain research, neuroscience, and the examination of human discernment. These states challenge our regular comprehension of the limits of awareness and brief inquiries concerning the connection between emotional encounters and objective reality.

With regards to shamanic rehearses and customary native conviction frameworks, the investigation of modified conditions of cognizance takes on a focal job. Professionals portray encounters in which they enter equal real factors to acquire bits of knowledge, get mending, and speak with soul elements. These encounters hold profound social and otherworldly importance and are viewed as a way to get to information and mending from inconspicuous domains.

The idea of equal real factors likewise tracks down reverberation in different social and profound customs all over the planet. Native conviction frameworks frequently integrate interconnected aspects and equal universes possessed by spirits, precursors, and extraordinary creatures. These convictions advance comprehension we might interpret assorted cosmologies and the manners by which various societies see the texture of the real world.

In the domain of imaginative articulation and narrating, the idea of equal universes has been a wellspring of motivation for creators, producers, and craftsmen. Sci-fi stories have investigated the outcomes of substitute real factors, going from universes where history took an alternate course to universes with fundamentally modified actual regulations. These inventive works welcome us to ponder the effect of decisions, the pliability of history, and the potential outcomes of assorted real factors.

The idea of substitute real factors has prompted the production of intriguing stories that act as mirrors to our own reality, provoking us to consider our qualities, decisions, and the outcomes of our activities. By investigating the "reflect universe," where recognizable characters and substances exist in an equal reality with differentiating virtues and inspirations, we are tested to reconsider how we might interpret human instinct and the effect of our choices.

All in all, the mission to find proof of substitute real factors through equal universes is an excursion that traverses the domains of science, reasoning, human cognizance, and imaginative articulation. It welcomes us to examine the idea of the real world, the interconnectedness of quantum occasions, and the boundless variety of presence. The idea of equal universes challenges our customary comprehension of a solitary and direct reality, making the way for a multiverse of potential outcomes.

While the Many-Universes Understanding remaining parts a subject of discussion and investigation, it has roused scientists to examine quantum peculiarities, entrapment, and enormous microwave foundation radiation for backhanded proof of equal universes. The inflationary multiverse speculation in cosmology has extended how we might interpret the universe's beginnings and its likely association with a more extensive multiverse structure.

In the domain of quantum figuring, the idea of equal universes thely affects encryption and information security, prompting the improvement of post-quantum cryptography. Modified conditions of awareness, shamanic rehearses, and native conviction frameworks challenge how we might interpret human discernment and the limits of the real world.

Equal universes have likewise been a wellspring of imaginative motivation, leading to provocative stories and investigations of substitute real factors in writing and mainstream society. These accounts act as mirrors to our own reality, empowering us.

9.1 Reflection on the enduring impact of parallel worlds

The idea of equal universes, otherwise called substitute real factors or the multiverse, has made a permanent imprint on human idea, creative mind, and logical request. As we consider the persevering through effect of equal universes, we end up brought into a domain where the limits of the truth are obscured, and the conceivable outcomes of presence are extended past ordinary cutoff points. This investigation has penetrated different areas of human information, from material science and reasoning to writing and workmanship, molding the manner in which we see the world and our place inside it.

The persevering through interest with equal universes lies in its capacity to challenge the actual substance of how we might interpret reality. It urges us to scrutinize the idea of presence, the job of decision, and the interconnectedness of occasions. It prompts us to consider the immeasurability of conceivable outcomes that could unfurl in the tremendous scene of the multiverse.

One of the focal hypothetical systems related with equal universes is the Many-Universes Translation (MWI) of quantum mechanics. Proposed by Hugh Everett III in 1957, the MWI recommends that each quantum occasion brings about the stretching of the universe into numerous equal universes, each addressing an alternate result of the occasion.

In this understanding, particles exist in superpositions of states until noticed, and each conceivable result of a quantum occasion happens in a different part of the multiverse.

The ramifications of the MWI venture into the core of quantum reality and challenge our regular comprehension of the job of perception in forming the course of occasions. It proposes a reality where each decision, activity, and estimation prompts the production of equal universes, each with its extraordinary arrangement of results. This point of view welcomes us to consider the significant meaning of our decisions and activities in reality as we know it where the stretching of truths is a key part of presence.

The MWI has not exclusively been a subject of discussion and investigation in the domain of hypothetical physical science yet has likewise found reverberation in the fields of quantum figuring and quantum data science. Quantum PCs outfit the capability of quantum superposition to perform estimations in various states all the while, offering the commitment of remarkable computational speedup for specific assignments.

The idea of quantum figuring in equal universes brings up issues about its effect on encryption and information security. Quantum PCs can possibly break customary encryption techniques, provoking our capacity to safeguard delicate data in our current reality where equal real factors and quantum superposition are a reality. This situation has provoked specialists and specialists to foster new encryption methods and safety efforts to defend information and correspondences in a quantum world.

While the MWI stays a subject of continuous exploration and discussion, it has motivated researchers to investigate peculiarities, for example, quantum trap and grandiose microwave foundation radiation for circuitous proof of equal universes. Quantum snare, a peculiarity in which particles become corresponded so that the condition of one molecule is subject to the condition of another, has prompted the speculation that ensnared particles in our universe might be associated with their partners in other equal universes.

Trial of quantum snare and the infringement of Chime disparities have given interesting experiences into the idea of quantum reality and the possible presence of equal universes. These trials have looked to resolve inquiries concerning the non-nearby way of behaving of trapped particles and the ramifications for how we might interpret quantum mechanics.

The investigation of vast microwave foundation radiation (CMB), the phosphorescence of the Enormous detonation, has likewise been a road for investigating proof of equal universes. Speculations recommend that the CMB could convey engraves from collaborations or impacts between our universe and equal universes, leaving perceptible marks in the radiation. While research in this space is continuous, no authoritative proof has arisen to help this speculation.

In the domain of cosmology, the idea of the multiverse has become laced with the hypothesis of astronomical expansion. Grandiose expansion suggests that the universe went through a quick and dramatic extension not long after the Enormous detonation. This hypothesis, upheld by different galactic perceptions, has led to the idea of an "inflationary multiverse."

As per the inflationary multiverse speculation, various areas of the universe might have encountered fluctuating paces of expansion, prompting the development of air pocket like spaces with particular actual properties. Every one of these air pocket spaces could address a different universe with its own arrangement of actual regulations and occasions. The inflationary multiverse gives a system to the age of equal universes inside a more extensive multiverse structure.

While the inflationary multiverse speculation stays speculative and dependent upon continuous exploration and discussion, it has extended how we might interpret the starting points of the universe and the likely associations between our existence and a more extensive multiverse. It welcomes us to think about how conceivable it is that the universe we possess is only one among many, each with its one of a kind qualities and history.

The investigation of equal universes stretches out past the limits of logical request and pervades different parts of human culture and innovativeness. Writing, specifically, has been a rich ground for the improvement of stories that investigate the results of substitute real factors. Sci-fi writers and narrators have created convincing stories that welcome perusers to mull over the ramifications of various decisions, adjusted narratives, and different actual regulations.

In the domain of writing and mainstream society, the idea of equal universes has led to endless imaginative accounts. These stories act as a focal point through which we can look at the outcomes of decisions, moral choices, and cultural designs. The idea of the "reflect universe," an equal reality where recognizable characters and substances exist with differentiating virtues and inspirations, challenges how we might interpret human instinct and the effect of our decisions.

A great representation of the "reflect universe" idea can be viewed as in the "Star Trip" establishment, which has investigated the possibility of an equal reality in a few of its series. In these stories, watchers are given a universe where natural characters take on changed jobs and moral arrangements. This story gadget urges us to ponder the impact of decisions, morals, and virtues in forming the course of history and individual fates.

The getting through effect of equal universes additionally stretches out into the domain of reasoning and transcendentalism. Savants have examined inquiries regarding the idea of the real world, the presence of numerous aspects, and the connection between the noticed and the unseen. The idea of equal universes challenges conventional philosophical systems and energizes a reexamination of how we might interpret presence.

In the domain of human cognizance, the investigation of changed conditions of mindfulness has been firmly associated with the idea of equal real factors. Practices like contemplation, hallucinogenic encounters, and tactile hardship have offered people the chance to see substitute aspects, experience creatures from equal real factors, and excursion into strange scenes of the psyche.

These encounters have tested how we might interpret human discernment and the limits of awareness. They brief us to think about the connection between emotional encounters and objective reality, as people portray experiences with substitute aspects and equal creatures during changed conditions of mindfulness.

The idea of equal real factors has additionally tracked down reverberation in different social and profound customs. Native conviction frameworks frequently consolidate interconnected aspects and equal universes occupied by spirits, progenitors, and heavenly creatures. These convictions improve how we might interpret assorted cosmologies and the manners by which various societies see the texture of the real world.

As we think about the getting through effect of equal universes, it becomes apparent that the idea rises above the limits of individual trains and saturates different features of human information, creative mind, and investigation. Whether in the domains of science, reasoning, writing, or social conviction frameworks, equal universes fills in as a strong impetus for extending our viewpoints and testing our predispositions about the idea of the real world.

The persevering through interest with equal universes lies in its capacity to grow how we might interpret presence and urge us to consider the significant interconnectedness of occasions and decisions. It advises us that each choice, each activity, and each estimation might prompt the making of equal universes, each with its extraordinary arrangement of results.

In the field of quantum registering, the idea of quantum superposition offers the commitment of progressive headways in computational capacities. Quantum PCs influence the capability of equal handling by performing computations in different states all the while. This capacity holds the possibility to change fields like cryptography, advancement, and recreations.

The improvement of quantum processing brings up issues about the effect on encryption and information security in reality as we know it where equal real factors and quantum superposition are a reality. The capacity of quantum PCs to break customary encryption techniques moves our ability to safeguard delicate data and correspondences. Accordingly, analysts and specialists are effectively growing new encryption strategies and safety efforts to address this test.

9.2 The significance of parallel worlds in literature, science, and culture

Equal universes, otherwise called substitute real factors or the multiverse, play had a huge impact in shaping human idea, creative mind, and social articulation. This idea, which proposes the presence of numerous coinciding aspects or universes, has made a permanent imprint on writing, science, and different parts of human culture. As we investigate the meaning of equal universes in these spaces, we reveal the significant impact they have had on the manner in which we see reality, decide, and think about the human condition.

In writing, the idea of equal universes has been a wellspring of motivation for writers, offering rich ground for the improvement of creative stories that challenge the limits of the real world. Sci-fi, specifically, has embraced substitute real factors to investigate a large number of conceivable outcomes, from universes where history unfurled diversely to universes with fundamentally modified actual regulations.

Equal universes in writing frequently act as a material for writers to look at the outcomes of various decisions, moral choices, and cultural designs. These accounts welcome perusers to mull over the ramifications of adjusted narratives and the flexibility of the human experience. One of the focal topics investigated is the "reflect universe," an equal reality where recognizable characters and elements exist with differentiating virtues, inspirations, and results.

A perfect representation of the "reflect universe" idea can be viewed as in the "Star Journey" establishment, which has investigated the possibility of an equal reality in a few of its series. In these stories, watchers are given a universe where notable characters from the "Star Journey" universe take on modified jobs and moral arrangements. This account gadget challenges how we might interpret human instinct and the impact of decisions and morals in molding the course of history and individual predeterminations.

The meaning of equal universes in writing lies in its capacity to act as a mirror to our own reality, provoking perusers to consider the effect of decisions, moral choices, and the results of activities. By inspecting substitute real factors, writing urges us to rethink our qualities, inspirations, and the interconnectedness of occasions.

Equal universes have likewise tracked down a significant spot in the domain of science and logical investigation. While the idea of substitute real factors stays speculative in mainstream researchers, it has motivated scientists to explore peculiarities and lead tests that could give backhanded proof of equal universes. One of the focal hypothetical structures related with equal universes is the Many-Universes Translation (MWI) of quantum mechanics.

The MWI, proposed by Hugh Everett III in 1957, recommends that each quantum occasion brings about the fanning of the universe into various equal universes, each addressing an alternate result of the occasion. In this translation, particles exist in superpositions of states until noticed, and each conceivable result of a quantum occasion happens in a different part of the multiverse.

This translation challenges our conventional comprehension of quantum mechanics, where particles are depicted as existing in a solitary state until noticed. It has significant ramifications for the idea of quantum reality and the job of perception in molding the course of occasions. The MWI proposes that each decision, activity, and estimation prompts the formation of equal universes, each with its interesting arrangement of results.

In the domain of quantum registering, the idea of equal universes affects encryption and information security. Quantum PCs influence the capability of quantum superposition to perform estimations in various states all the while, offering the commitment of outstanding computational speedup for specific assignments.

The capacity of quantum PCs to break conventional encryption techniques provokes our ability to safeguard delicate data and correspondences. Specialists are effectively growing new encryption strategies and safety efforts to address the security challenges presented by quantum registering in reality as we know it where equal real factors and quantum superposition are a reality.

The investigation of equal universes in the field of quantum mechanics has prompted the examination of peculiarities, for example, quantum entrapment and grandiose microwave foundation radiation for roundabout proof of equal universes. Quantum entrapment, a peculiarity in which particles become corresponded so that the condition of one molecule is subject to the condition of another, has led to the speculation that snared particles in our universe might be associated with their partners in other equal universes.

Exploratory trial of quantum trap and the infringement of Chime disparities have given captivating experiences into the idea of quantum reality and the likely presence of equal universes. These investigations try to resolve inquiries concerning the non-nearby way of behaving of snared particles and their associations across equal real factors.

The investigation of vast microwave foundation radiation (CMB), the glimmer of the Enormous detonation, has additionally been a road for investigating proof of equal universes. Speculations propose that the CMB could convey engraves from communications or crashes between our universe and equal universes, leaving distinguishable marks in the radiation. While research in this space is continuous, no authoritative proof has arisen to help this theory.

In cosmology, the idea of the multiverse is entwined with the hypothesis of grandiose expansion. Vast expansion suggests that the universe went through a fast and outstanding extension not long after the Enormous detonation. This hypothesis, upheld by different galactic perceptions, has led to the thought of an "inflationary multiverse."

As per the inflationary multiverse speculation, various districts of the universe might have encountered shifting paces of expansion, prompting the arrangement of air pocket like spaces with particular actual properties. Every one of these air pocket spaces could address a different universe with its own arrangement of actual regulations and occasions. The inflationary multiverse gives a system to the age of equal universes inside a more extensive multiverse structure.

While the inflationary multiverse speculation stays speculative and is dependent upon continuous exploration and discussion, it has developed how we might interpret the starting points of the universe and the expected associations between our world and a more extensive multiverse. It welcomes us to think about how conceivable it is that the universe we possess is only one among many, each with its exceptional attributes and history.

The investigation of equal universes has likewise tracked down reverberation in the domain of human cognizance and changed conditions of mindfulness. Practices like contemplation, hallucinogenic encounters, and tangible hardship have offered people the chance to see substitute aspects, experience creatures from equal real factors, and excursion into strange scenes of the psyche.

These encounters have tested how we might interpret human insight and the limits of awareness. They brief us to consider the connection between abstract encounters and objective reality as people portray experiences with substitute aspects and equal creatures during adjusted conditions of mindfulness.

With regards to shamanic rehearses and conventional native conviction frameworks, the investigation of changed conditions of cognizance takes on a focal job. Experts portray encounters in which they enter equal real factors to acquire experiences, get mending, and speak with soul substances. These excursions into modified conditions of cognizance hold profound social and otherworldly importance and are viewed as a way to get to information and mending from inconspicuous domains.

The idea of equal real factors additionally tracks down reverberation in different social and profound practices. Native conviction frameworks frequently integrate interconnected aspects and equal universes possessed by spirits, predecessors, and otherworldly creatures. These convictions improve how we might interpret assorted cosmologies and the manners by which various societies see the texture of the real world.

All in all, the meaning of equal universes in writing, science, and culture is a demonstration of their getting through influence on human idea and creative mind. In writing, equal universes have roused imaginative stories that investigate the outcomes of various decisions, modified chronicles, and different cultural designs. These stories act as a mirror to our own reality, empowering us to rethink our qualities, inspirations, and the interconnectedness of occasions.

In the domain of science, the idea of equal universes has prompted the examination of quantum peculiarities, quantum entrapment, and grandiose microwave foundation radiation in the quest for roundabout proof of equal universes. The investigation of the multiverse has developed how we might interpret quantum mechanics, cosmology, and the expected associations between our universe and a more extensive multiverse.

Equal universes have additionally made a permanent imprint in the domain of human cognizance and changed conditions of mindfulness. Practices like contemplation, hallucinogenic encounters, and shamanic ventures challenge how we might interpret human discernment and brief us to think about the connection between abstract encounters and objective reality.

The idea of equal real factors has tracked down reverberation in different social and profound practices, improving comprehension we might interpret assorted cosmologies and the interconnected aspects possessed by spirits, predecessors, and powerful creatures.

9.3 Encouraging further exploration and contemplation of alternate realities

The investigation of substitute real factors, equal universes, and the multiverse is an excursion that welcomes us to rise above the limits of our ongoing comprehension and investigate the boundless embroidery of presence. It flashes interest, animates imagination, and difficulties our view of reality in significant ways. As we energize further investigation and thought of substitute real factors, we end up setting out on a journey that incorporates science, reasoning, workmanship, and the human creative mind.

In the domain of science, the idea of equal universes has opened ways to new boondocks of investigation. The Many-Universes Translation (MWI) of quantum mechanics, proposed by Hugh Everett III, has catalyzed conversations and tests that look to give proof to the presence of equal universes. While the MWI stays a subject of discussion, it has enlivened researchers to dive into quantum peculiarities, quantum snare, and infinite microwave foundation radiation for expected indications of equal real factors.

Quantum snare, a peculiarity where particles become corresponded such that the condition of one molecule relies upon the condition of another, has led to the charming speculation that caught particles in our universe might have associations with their partners in other equal universes. Trial of quantum snare and the infringement of Chime imbalances have looked to unwind the secrets of quantum reality and investigate the chance of equal universes.

The investigation of enormous microwave foundation radiation (CMB), the phosphorescence of the Huge explosion, has offered a remarkable road for looking for proof of equal universes. Speculations recommend that the CMB might convey engraves from communications or impacts between our universe and equal universes, leaving perceivable marks in the radiation. While no authoritative proof has arisen to help these speculations, specialists proceed to research and investigate the enormous microwave foundation for pieces of information about the presence of equal real factors.

In cosmology, the hypothesis of grandiose expansion has presented the idea of the inflationary multiverse, where various areas of the universe experienced fluctuating paces of expansion, leading to bubble-like spaces with particular actual properties. Every one of these air pocket spaces could address a different universe with its own arrangement of actual regulations and occasions. This speculation has extended how we might interpret the universe's starting points and its possible association with a more extensive multiverse structure.

The investigation of substitute real factors reaches out to the field of quantum registering, where the idea of quantum superposition offers the commitment of note-worthy progressions in computational abilities. Quantum PCs, with their capacity to perform computations in different states all the while, can possibly alter fields like cryptography, improvement, and reenactments.

The improvement of quantum processing brings up issues about the effect on en-cryption and information security in our current reality where equal real factors and quantum superposition are a reality. Quantum PCs can possibly break conventional encryption techniques, representing a critical test to our capacity to safeguard delicate data and correspondences. Scientists and specialists are effectively growing new en-cryption procedures and safety efforts to address this test and shield information in a quantum world.

The idea of substitute real factors has not just made some meaningful difference in the domain of science yet has likewise tracked down a profound reverberation in the realm of human cognizance and changed conditions of mindfulness. Practices like contemplation, hallucinogenic encounters, and shamanic ventures offer people the potential chance to see substitute aspects, experience creatures from equal real factors, and investigate the strange scenes of the brain.

These encounters challenge how we might interpret human discernment and the limits of cognizance. They brief us to consider the connection between abstract encounters and objective reality as people depict experiences with substitute aspects and equal creatures during adjusted conditions of mindfulness.

Shamanic rehearses and conventional native conviction frameworks integrate the idea of interconnected aspects and equal universes possessed by spirits, precursors, and extraordinary creatures.

These convictions offer a rich embroidery of cosmologies and perspectives that improve how we might interpret different social viewpoints and the interconnected texture of the real world.

The getting through meaning of substitute real factors in writing can't be put into words. Sci-fi, specifically, has embraced the idea to create inventive stories that stretch the limits of the real world. These stories act as mirrors to our own reality, welcoming perusers to think about the outcomes of various decisions, moral choices, and cultural designs.

The idea of the "reflect universe," where recognizable characters and substances exist in an equal reality with differentiating virtues and inspirations, challenges how we might interpret human instinct and the effect of our decisions. Sci-fi writing urges us to consider the potential outcomes that emerge from different real factors, unique narratives, and modified actual regulations.

As we support further investigation and thought of substitute real factors, it is fundamental to perceive the significant effect of these ideas on our perspectives, scholarly interest, and imaginative articulations. This investigation rises above the limits of logical request and pervades the domains of reasoning, workmanship, and social conviction frameworks.

The mission to comprehend substitute real factors prompts us to consider central inquiries concerning the idea of presence, the meaning of decision, and the limitlessness of conceivable outcomes that could unfurl in the multiverse. It challenges our traditional comprehension of a solitary, straight reality and urges us to embrace the possibility that various aspects or universes might coincide close by our own.

In the domain of reasoning, the investigation of substitute real factors difficulties customary systems and supports a reconsideration of how we might interpret presence. It prompts us to examine the interconnectedness of occasions, the job of decision, and the effect of our activities in our current reality where each choice prompts the production of equal universes.

The meaning of substitute real factors additionally reaches out into the domain of craftsmanship and imagination. Specialists, journalists, and makers have drawn motivation from the idea of equal universes to create provocative stories, visual fine arts, and vivid encounters. These imaginative articulations act for of investigating the human condition, considering the outcomes of decisions, and rousing crowds to ponder the unlimited potential outcomes of presence.

The persevering through meaning of equal universes lies in their ability to extend how we might interpret the interconnectedness of occasions, the job of decision, and the tremendousness of potential outcomes. This idea fills in as a scaffold between logical investigation and creative articulation, cultivating a more profound association between the domains of reason and creative mind.

As we support further investigation and consideration of substitute real factors, we are setting out on an excursion that rises above the limits of information and reaches out into the unknown regions of the human creative mind and the actual universe. The journey to comprehend equal universes rouses scholarly interest, invigorates inventiveness, and difficulties our assumptions about the idea of the real world.